PEMBROKESHIRE
COAST PATH

PEMBROKESHIRE COAST PATH

Brian John

Photographs by Martin Trelawney
General editor Michael Allaby

AURUM PRESS

COUNTRYSIDE COMMISSION · ORDNANCE SURVEY

ACKNOWLEDGEMENTS

Walking the full length of the Pembrokeshire Coast Path for this book has brought me very great pleasure, and I hope that those who use the book to help them in their own explorations will sense something of this in my text. There are a number of people to thank: first, my wife Inger, who has helped on most of my outings; Sally Rudman for help with typing; Peter Hordley and David Matthews of the Pembrokeshire Coast National Park Authority, and especially their colleague Tom Goodall for much invaluable assistance and information; Stephen Evans of the NCC, for information on coastal natural history; and John Barrett, whose HMSO/Countryside Commission guide of 1974 has been an invaluable companion. I have also learnt much from David Saunders, Robert Kennedy, Roger Worsley, Dillwyn Miles, Pat Wolseley, and Richard Howells. Finally, I thank Michael Allaby, the editor of the national trail guides, for his encouragement while I have worked under some pressure to walk the path and write the book.

Brian John is a Pembrokeshire man and a geographer by training. He lectured at Durham University for 11 years before returning to Pembrokeshire, where he now runs his own small publishing company. He is also greatly involved in local environmental and conservation organisations.

This edition first published 1990 by Aurum Press Ltd in association with the Countryside Commission and the Ordnance Survey
Text copyright © 1990 by Aurum Press Ltd, the Countryside Commission and the Ordnance Survey
Maps Crown copyright © 1990 by the Ordnance Survey
Photographs copyright © 1990 by the Countryside Commission

British Library Cataloguing in Publication Data

John, Brian
Pembrokeshire Coast Path. – (National trail guides; 7)
1. Coastal regions. Long-distance footpaths:
Pembrokeshire Coast Path. Visitors' guides
I. Title   II. Allaby, Michael 1933–   III. Series
914.29'62.

ISBN 1 85410 023 8
OS ISBN 0 319 00193 8

Book design by Robert Updegraff
Cover photograph: Freshwater West
Title page photograph: the secluded cove of Aber Bach (Hescwm), near Dinas

Typeset by Wyvern Typesetting Ltd, Bristol
Printed and bound in Italy by Printers Srl, Trento

CONTENTS

Circular walks appear on pages 42, 64, 94, 104, 130 and 146

How to use this guide

This guide to the 181-mile (292-kilometre) Pembrokeshire Coast Path is in three parts:

- The introduction, with an historical background to the area and advice for walkers.
- The Coast Path itself, split into twelve chapters, with maps opposite the description for each route section. The distances noted with each chapter represent the total walking length of the Pembrokeshire Coast Path, including sections through towns and villages. There may be some variation, depending on whether firing ranges are open. This part of the guide also includes information on places of interest as well as a number of short walks which can be taken around each part of the path. Key sites are numbered both in the text and on the maps to make it easier to follow the route description.
- The last part includes useful information, such as local transport, accommodation and organisations involved with the Pembrokeshire Coast Path.

The maps have been prepared by the Ordnance Survey for this trail guide using 1:25 000 Pathfinder or Outdoor Leisure maps as a base. The line of the Pembrokeshire Coast Path is shown in yellow, with the status of each section of the trail – footpath or bridleway, for example – shown in green underneath (see key on inside front cover). These rights of way markings also indicate the precise alignment of the Pembrokeshire Coast Path, which walkers should follow. In some cases, the yellow line on these maps may show a route that is different from that shown on older maps; walkers are recommended to follow the yellow route in this guide, which will be the route that is waymarked with the distinctive acorn symbol ♣ used for all national trails. Any parts of the Pembrokeshire Coast Path that may be difficult to follow on the ground are clearly highlighted in the route description, and important points to watch for are marked with letters in each chapter, both in the text and on the maps. *Some maps start on a right-hand page and continue on the left-hand page – black arrows (➡) at the edge of the maps indicate the start point.*

Should there be a need to divert the Pembrokeshire Coast Path from the route shown in this guide, for maintenance work or because the route has had to be changed, walkers are advised to follow any waymarks or signs along the path.

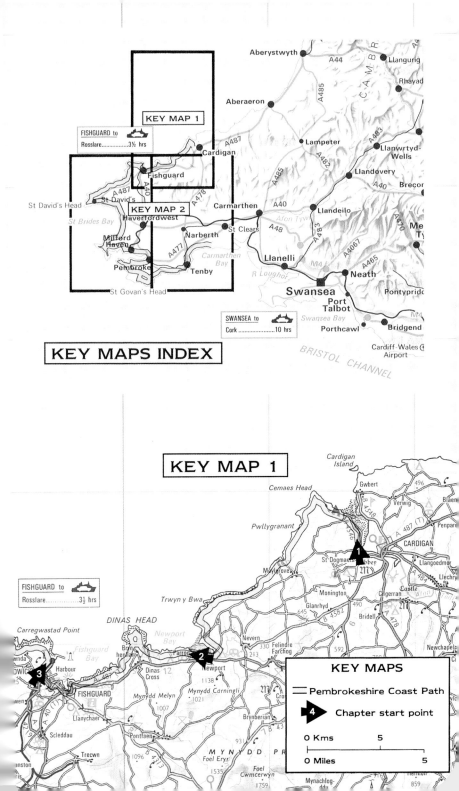

KEY MAPS INDEX

KEY MAP 1

FISHGUARD to Rosslare.................3½ hrs

KEY MAP 2

SWANSEA to Cork ....10 hrs

KEY MAP 1

FISHGUARD to Rosslare.................3½ hrs

KEY MAPS

— Pembrokeshire Coast Path

◀ Chapter start point

0 Kms — 5

0 Miles — 5

Distance checklist

This list will assist you in calculating the distance between your proposed overnight accommodation and in checking your progress along the walk.

location	approx. distance from previous location	
	miles	km
St Dogmaels	0	0
Poppit Sands	1.3	2.7
Ceibwr Bay (for Moylgrove 0.8 miles/1.3 km)	5.6	9.0
Newport (Parrog)	8.6	13.8
Cwm-yr-Eglwys	3.1	5.0
Fishguard (via Dinas Head)	7.0	11.3
Goodwick (Harbour Heights)	2.3	3.7
Aber Bach (for St Nicholas 1.4 miles/2.3 km)	11.5	18.5
Abercastle	3.3	5.3
Trefin	2.7	4.3
Porth-gain	1.7	2.7
Whitesands Bay	9.5	15.3
Porth Clais (for St David's 1.1 miles/1.8 km)	6.5	10.5
Solva	5.8	9.3
Newgale	4.8	7.7
Nolton Haven (for Nolton 0.6 miles/1.0 km)	3.0	4.8
Broad Haven	3.5	5.6
Little Haven	0.8	1.3
St Bride's Haven	5.4	8.7
Musselwick (for Marloes 0.7 miles/1.1 km)	2.3	3.7
Marloes Sands (for Marloes 1.3 miles/2.1 km)	4.8	7.7
Dale (via St Ann's Head)	7.8	12.6
Monk Haven (for St Ishmael's 0.7 miles/1.1 km)	2.5	4.0 via Pickleridge
	4.7*	7.6 via Mullock Bridge
(Sandy Haven) East side of Sandy Haven Pill (for Herbrandston 0.9 miles/1.4 kms)	3.6	5.8 via stepping stones
	7.4*	11.9 via Rickeston Bridge and Herbrandston
Hakin	3.9	6.3
Milford Haven	0.7	1.1
Neyland	5.3	8.5
Pembroke Dock	3.4	5.5

Pembroke	2.8	4.5	
Angle	11.3	18.2	
Castlemartin	10.5	16.9	
Bosherston	5.0*	8.0	via Sampson Cross
	7.5	12.1	via Stack Rocks and St Govan's Chapel
Freshwater East (0.6 miles/1.0 km to village)	6.9*	11.1	via lily pools to Broad Haven
	9.1	14.6	via St Govan's Head to Broad Haven
(Castlemartin to Freshwater East via St Govan's Head, avoiding Bosherston 10.3* miles/16.6 km)			
Manorbier Bay (for Manorbier 0.4 miles/0.6 km)	3.7	6.0	
Lydstep Haven (for Lydstep 0.4 miles/0.6 km)	4.1	6.6	
Penally	2.4	3.9	via A4139
	3.6*	5.8	via Giltar Point
Tenby	2.1	3.4	
Saundersfoot	4.1	6.6	
Wiseman's Bridge	1.3	2.1	
Amroth	1.9	3.1	

* = not used for overall distance

The wreck of a Greek tug beneath the cliffs at Porth y Rhaw.

PREFACE

The Pembrokeshire Coast Path is one of the national trails in England and Wales that the Countryside Commission promotes for walkers – and, in the case of some trails, riders – to explore and enjoy the best of our countryside, far away from towns, traffic and the bustle of urban life.

These trails are particularly suited for long journeys, but they can also be sampled on an afternoon or over a weekend. Another way of using them is as part of a round trip, or circular walk, and suggestions for these are included in this guide. National trails are maintained by local or national park authorities on behalf of the Commission, and are well waymarked with our distinctive acorn. Each trail provides an enjoyable, and sometimes challenging, walk or ride in the countryside.

National trails run through the grandest and most beautiful countryside and coast which England and Wales have to offer. Many of them also link with other waymarked paths, thus making it possible to plan a variety of journeys throughout the countryside.

We hope you will enjoy walking along the Pembrokeshire Coast Path and that this guide will help to make your journey one to remember.

Derek Barber

Sir Derek Barber
Chairman
Countryside Commission

PART ONE

INTRODUCTION

Introducing the Pembrokeshire coast

The Pembrokeshire Coast Path was designated as a national trail in order to allow free public access to one of Europe's most magnificent and varied coastlines. Where possible, the route runs close to the cliff edge; but this is by no means a simple cliffed coast and there are stretches that run along, or close to, sandy beaches; stretches far enough inland to be out of sight and sound of the sea; and stretches on the shores of the deep natural harbour of Milford Haven. On every section of the footpath you will encounter creeks, coves, coastal valleys and sandy beaches, and you are seldom far from civilisation. Indeed, the string of little coastal villages discovered at regular intervals by the Coast Path walker gives this coastline much of its charm, adding a sense of scale, intimacy and warmth to cliff scenery that might otherwise be somewhat intimidating.

The landscape of Pembrokeshire is immensely ancient. All of the rocks underlying the land surface are more than 300 million years old, and in the cliffs you can see in varying colours, textures and patterns, the story of Britain's evolution over some 700 million years of geological time. The relations between rocks and cliff scenery are described in more detail on page 32. Here and there the events of the Ice Age have dramatically affected the coastline, with the creation of deep valleys and the dumping of glacial and other sediments.

For the most part the inland landscape, truncated by the coastal cliffs, is flat or gently undulating, and these ancient platform surfaces have themselves been partly fashioned by the work of the sea at times of higher sea levels millions of years ago. In places the youngest platforms, around 100 feet (30 metres) above the present sea level, are quite spectacular – as around Flimston, on the southern limestone coast, or in the Marloes–Dale area. Elsewhere, the old platforms have been modified by river action and given a gently undulating appearance. And in other areas, especially in the north, the uplands of Pembrokeshire extend right out to the coast, giving rise to cliffs over 330 feet (100 metres) high.

The wildlife of Pembrokeshire is superb, and indeed it is because of the wonderful displays of spring wild flowers and the abundance of sea birds that this coastal environment is so greatly valued. The Pembrokeshire air is clean, the light is clear, and the water has a blueness that never ceases to amaze visitors from the North Sea coasts. All of the coastal cliff tops are transformed in the months of April, May and June by sheets of wild flowers, and at the same time sea birds are nesting in their thousands – for the most part on the offshore islands but also to an increasing extent on mainland cliffs. Later in the year the wildlife is less abundant and the colours less exotic, but walking the path during the high summer months is an experience to be treasured none the less.

In this guide I have tried to emphasise the great variety of natural features and wildlife to be seen along the coast, but we must not forget the human influence, which is everywhere apparent. This is – and has been for many centuries – a farmed landscape. The twin activities of farming and fishing have provided the staples of the local diet until very recently. The coastal settlements were the focal points of Pembrokeshire life, for the sea was above all a provider of food. But it was also the major highway before the arrival of good road and rail communications about a century ago. There are many reminders of this maritime tradition – the cromlechs of the Neolithic folk who arrived by sea, the promontory forts of the Iron Age immigrants, the churches and chapels of the seafaring Celtic saints and their followers, the coastal castles of the Norman invaders, and the Victorian defences built to repel a French invasion force that never arrived. The little quays, lime kilns, breakwaters and warehouses that feature prominently in the coastal settlements remind us also of the long tradition of shipbuilding and coastal trading which has now been overtaken by the new tradition of seafaring for fun.

One cultural feature that will be immediately apparent to the observant map-reading coastal walker is the predominance of Welsh place names in the north, contrasting with the predominance of English place names in the south. And scattered along the whole of the Pembrokeshire coast are Scandinavian names adding spice to the mixture – for example, Ramsey, Skomer, Grassholm, Musselwick, Hubberston and Gosker. The Welsh–English split is a matter of early medieval history, owing its origins to the successful colonisation of South Pembrokeshire by the Normans and their followers, and the successful resistance of the Welsh inhabitants of the north. For more than 900 years the two communities have lived side by side more or less amicably. The divide or *Landsker*, which separated them in the Middle Ages, is still in more or less its original position, and still traceable.

The Industrial Revolution came late to Pembrokeshire and had an impact only in small coastal pockets. Places such as Porthgain, Abereiddi, Pembroke Dock and Wiseman's Bridge still bear its scars, but the impact of the coal era has been lessened over time as the little mines and spoil heaps of the Pembrokeshire coalfield have been reduced to fragmentary ruins and grassy mounds. The latest episodes in Pembrokeshire's history still make dramatic impacts on the landscape. For example, the Milford Haven oil industry has developed over the last 30 years on a scale out of all proportion to anything that has gone before. But nothing is for ever. Already two of the installations have closed, and there is no knowing how long the others will survive. The holiday industry, too, waxes and wanes as tastes and economic circumstances change. Caravan parks, self-catering chalets, marinas and leisure parks are now essential features of the Pembrokeshire scene. Who knows how long they will last? The coastal communities have seen it all before. Over centuries of change they have adapted and survived on this fascinating interface between land and sea that we know as the Pembrokeshire coast.

History of the Coast Path

The Pembrokeshire Coast Path was officially opened on 16th May 1970 by Wynford Vaughan Thomas, then President of the Council for the Protection of Rural Wales. Following the designation of the Pembrokeshire Coast National Park in 1952, the author and naturalist Ronald Lockley surveyed a route for a long-distance footpath following the coast, and his report for the Countryside Commission was enthusiastically accepted and acted upon in the summer of 1953. There were immense complications in designating the path; some sections were on existing rights of way, but the great majority of the coastline was, of course, in private hands, and hundreds of new rights of way had to be negotiated with individual landowners. The great majority of them were cooperative, and agreed to public access as long as new fences, walls and stiles could be built to prevent any undue disturbance to local farming activities. In many cases

The holy well at St Non's, near St David's, reputed to be the birthplace of the patron saint.

Rocky outcrops projecting through the sandy beach at Freshwater West, on the

...est-facing coast of the Castlemartin peninsula.

The lifeboat station at St Justinian's. Ramsey Island can be seen on the skyline.

farmers actually benefited from the improvement of clifftop fencing, and from the addition of steps and bridges in awkward locations. Some landowners proved difficult to deal with, and to this day there are a few places where the footpath heads unexpectedly away from the coast or sends the walker off on a convoluted detour. In many places the path had to be hacked out of the 'jungle' or created with the help of a miniature bulldozer. More than 100 footbridges were built, 479 numbered stiles installed, thousands of steps cut into steep and slippery slopes, dangerous cliff sections avoided and marked, and fingerposts erected; and landowners and members of the public were reassured that all of this 'damage' was in a good cause. Not surprisingly, these tasks took 17 years to complete.

Inevitably, the path still has its problem areas. Now, since the completion of the Cleddau Bridge across Milford Haven, it is possible to walk from St Dogmaels to Amroth without a break. But the Coast Path is not continuous. It was not designated through the built-up areas of Milford Haven, Neyland, Pembroke Dock, Pembroke, Tenby and Saundersfoot, and there are still long and frustrating detours around the Castlemartin Range, Manorbier Range, Penally Camp and Pembroke power station. In some places the path was never actually constructed along its designated route; elsewhere stretches of the marked route have proved unacceptable to walkers and they have made new routes of their own.

Now that the Coast Path is 20 years old it is inevitable that some rationalisation should occur. Its designated length is 167 miles (269 km), but since 1970 a number of Footpath Diversion Orders have lengthened it, and other changes are in the pipeline. For all practical purposes its length is now 181 miles (292 km). The National Park Authority, together with the district councils of Preseli Pembrokeshire and South Pembrokeshire, is waymarking the urban routes with pavement acorn symbols. Thus, in cooperation with Mr Tom Goodall of the National Park Authority, I have tried to identify the most direct and most logical urban routes for the long-distance walker. These recommended routes are published for the first time in this guide. If you enjoy and explore the Pembrokeshire coast properly, and visit the peninsulas of Lydstep Head, Dinas Island, St Govan's Head, and the Deer Park at Martin's Haven, you will actually walk in excess of 200 miles (320 km). Try not to miss out on any of it; the beautiful Pembrokeshire coast is quite incomparable.

Planning your walk and accommodation

Walking the Pembrokeshire Coast Path *can* be completed in under a week if you are in a great hurry, but such speed is not recommended! Better to take 12 days if you are fit and more if you are not. Remember that if you walk the whole route you will climb over 30,000 feet (9,150 metres) in the process. If you really want to enjoy the path, return to it again and again, savouring your favourite sections in different weathers and different seasons.

Sadly, I have to say that I do not recommend any complete sections of this path to disabled people, horseriders or cyclists. Steep slopes, dangerous proximity to the cliff edge, and frequent stiles mean that this is strictly a path for those who are reasonably fit, properly equipped and well shod. However, there are innumerable access points, in addition to those identified as the start/stop points at the beginning and end of each chapter of this book. Car parks, youth hostels, inns and other facilities are marked on the maps that follow.

If you are walking a long stretch of the route, which entails overnight stops, try to book accommodation or camping space beforehand, especially in the peak holiday months. Accommodation lists and other helpful leaflets can be obtained from tourist information centres or from the National Park Authority and district council tourism units.

Safety precautions

Conditions are not dangerous if you walk carefully and take proper account of weather conditions and the state of the ground underfoot; but remember that fatal accidents do occur on the cliffs of Pembrokeshire every year, usually because walkers take unnecessary risks and fail to appreciate that cliff tops and cliff faces are extremely dangerous. You are more likely to have an accident if you have a heavy pack and are extremely tired at the end of a long day. Make sure that somebody knows your walking plans and your estimated arrival time, especially outside the main holiday season; some stretches of the path are very isolated and access is difficult. Pay particular attention to those parts where cliff-falls and landslips are common; inevitably you will find that short sections of the path have been eroded away, leaving unmarked sheer drops that can be lethal if you are walking in bad light or heavy rain. If no detour has been established, then the national park rangers are probably unaware of the cliff-fall. Please make a note of the grid reference and inform the National Park Authority. Here and there you will encounter pits or crevasses in the footpath; usually they are signs of subsidence on the cliff edge. Beware of extreme wind turbulence, especially when there is an onshore wind blowing; on cliff tops, alternating powerful gusts and periods of calm can throw you off balance very quickly indeed. With the above points in mind, please be sure that dogs and children are kept under proper control. Never allow small children to run ahead of you or play games on clifftop sections of the Coast Path.

The weather encountered on the Pembrokeshire coast is nothing if not variable. It is always a good idea to carry a sweater, an anorak and a set of waterproofs. Wear good strong walking boots if you can afford them. And if you are walking alone, *always* carry a whistle and a bivouac sheet or some other protection in case you twist an ankle or suffer a more serious accident when you are in a remote spot.

A word about distances and tides. At Whitesands, Newgale, Broad Haven, Marloes, Freshwater West and Saundersfoot you can walk on the beach instead of the Coast Path if the tide is out; but carry a set of tide tables with you and do not allow yourself to be cut off by a rising tide. At the Gann (near Dale) and at Sandy Haven, delicate timing is needed in order to cross river mouths when the tide is low; if you get it wrong long detours are the inevitable penalty. The walk along the shore of Angle Bay can be uncomfortable at high tide.

Finally, good timing is also required if you want to walk the 'Range East' part of the Castlemartin Range. In general, the stretch from Stack Rocks to Broad Haven is open at weekends during the summer months, but on weekdays you may find it closed until 5 p.m. and face a very long walk on the road between Freshwater West and Bosherston. If you are lucky (or well organised) you may be able to join a guided walk with National Park staff along the cliff tops of Range West. Full information about firing schedules and access can be obtained either from the Range Office (tel. Castlemartin (064 681) 321) or from National Park information centres. Please note that there is *no* right of unaccompanied access to Range West at any time.

Do not be put off by any of the above. The path is not dangerous if you observe a few simple rules and, if you are well prepared and careful, you will enjoy the Pembrokeshire coast at its best.

PART TWO

PEMBROKESHIRE COAST PATH

1 St Dogmaels to Newport (Parrog)

passing Poppit Sands and Ceibwr Bay
15½ miles (25 km)

This stretch of the Pembrokeshire Coast Path is a taxing one, but walkers are amply rewarded for their efforts by continuous contact with wild and beautiful cliff scenery. Some of the highest cliffs in Pembrokeshire are encountered on this stretch, and walkers will climb more than 3,000 feet (915 metres) before they reach Newport. If you are not particularly fit, allow a good long day for this walk and assume that it will take you more than eight hours. Here, as elsewhere on the Pembrokeshire Coast Path, the route is well marked and well trodden, and there is little likelihood that you will go astray.

Cardigan **1** is well served by buses from all the neighbouring towns. To start on the trail proper, you need to get to the village of St Dogmaels, served by a regular bus service from Cardigan.

A view of the high cliff coast at Ceibwr Bay, with Pen yr Afr visible in the distance.

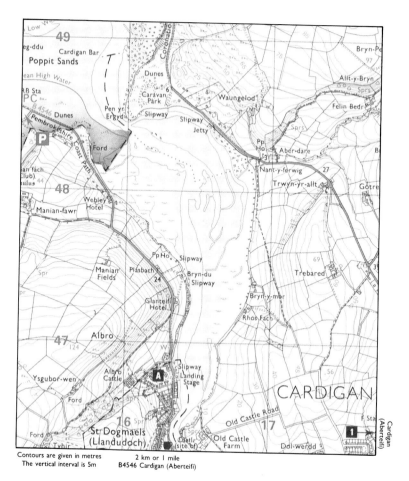

Contours are given in metres
The vertical interval is 5m

2 km or I mile

B4546 Cardigan (Aberteifi)

The unmarked start of the Pembrokeshire Coast Path **A** is adjacent to the landing stage at the northern end of St Dogmaels, an ancient fishing village whose houses cling to the steep hillsides above the Teifi Valley. The first 3 miles (4.5 km) of the route follow roads and country lanes. Once past Webley Hotel there are fine views of the shifting sands and mud banks of the estuary; to the west you can see the deep gash of the Cippyn channel cut across the headland by glacial meltwater about 200,000 years ago. The first sign for the 'Pembrokeshire Coast Long Distance Footpath' is on the wall at the roadside near the Poppit Sands shop/café. Dune repairs are in progress here, using marram grass. As the road climbs to over 425 feet (130 metres), you will have fine views across the estuary, towards Cardigan Island and around the full sweep of Cardigan Bay.

27

At Allt-y-goed Farm **B** you leave the country lane and start on the footpath. It is often wet and muddy near stile 478.

Cemaes Head **2** is a nature reserve managed by the Dyfed Wildlife Trust. The headland itself is low and unspectacular – the cliffs are much more impressive to the south of Craig yr Odyn, but as you round the head a wonderful vista opens up towards the south-west, with views of Dinas Island, Pen Caer and Strumble Head (look for the flashing light). The cliffs in this area are almost vertical and over 440 feet (135 metres) high. Continuing south along the path, you will pass the point at which the footpath leading back to Cnwcau or Cippyn leaves the Coast Path **C**.

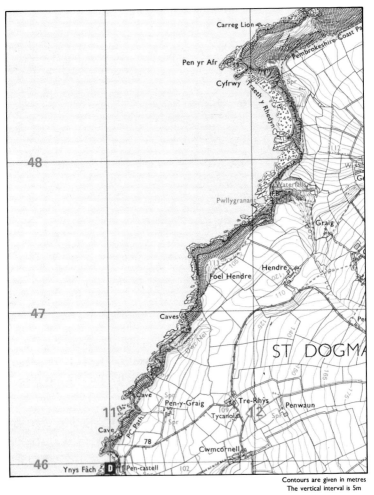

Contours are given in metres
The vertical interval is 5m

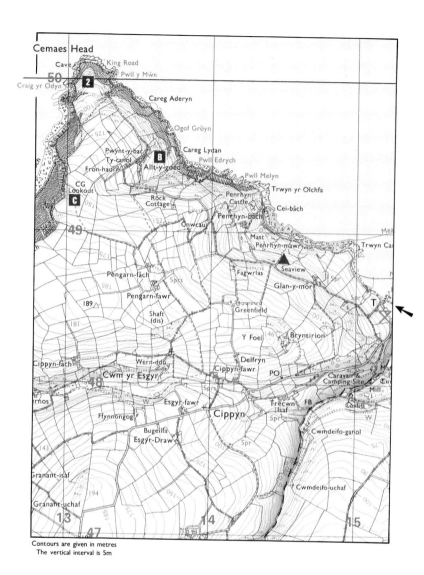

Contours are given in metres
The vertical interval is 5m

As you continue south-westwards you pass the highest point on the whole of the national trail – over 575 feet (175 metres). The cliffs are quite magnificent, revealing textbook examples of ancient folding and faulting structures in the rocks. You pass the pretty cove of Pwllygranant and eventually approach Ceibwr Bay. Watch for a footpath realignment **D**. You pass inland of Pen-castell, cross the lane and follow the edge of the field. Beware of boggy conditions as you descend into the valley.

Ceibwr **3** was once the port serving Moylgrove and the surrounding farming community. Note the ruined lime kiln near the mouth of the stream. The bay is now in the care of the National Trust. Fulmars nest on the cliffs here, and on several other cliff sections between Ceibwr and Newport. This bird is extending its range all the time along the Pembrokeshire coast; a century ago there was only one colony in the whole of Britain. There is also a breeding colony of house martins on the cliffs south of Ceibwr **3**.

Pwll y Wrach (the Witches Cauldron) **4** is one of the classic features of marine erosion on the Pembrokeshire coast. The cauldron itself is a collapsed cave, formed where the sea has been able to pick out soft crumbling shales and sandstones along a fault. There are steep gradients on both sides of the valley. Classic cliff scenery appears again in the great amphitheatre of cliffs looking down on the eastern end of Traeth Cell-Howel, where there are fine examples of rotational slumps with many thousands of tons of rock slipping downwards in a series of gigantic steps. The path here **E** is liable to disappear, so take care. Look to the *south* of the footpath and you will see that

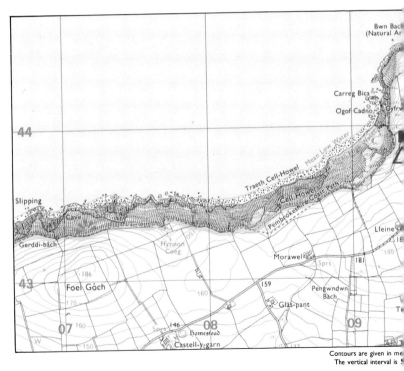

Contours are given in me
The vertical interval is !

a wide strip of land has dropped by at least 33 feet (10 metres). The fault scarps are clearly visible in the fields.

Follow the path for some 2½ miles (4 km) above the bevelled north-facing cliffs, walking for much of the time more than 500 feet (150 metres) above sea level. Down below there are a number of beaches used for breeding by Atlantic grey seals. On the flanks of the Trwyn y Bwa peninsula, look out for nesting fulmars, razorbills, guillemots and cormorants.

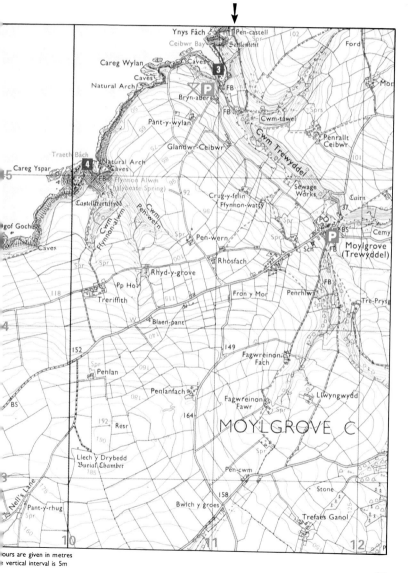

ours are given in metres
vertical interval is 5m

31

Morfa Head **5** provides glorious views across Newport Bay. As you descend southwards from the summit you pass through a rock garden of gorse and heather, one of many designated sites of special scientific interest on the coastal footpath.

Traeth Mawr ('Big Beach' or Newport Sands) is the best beach on the North Pembrokeshire coast. It has a good car park, surf lifesaving club, summer shop, toilets and a golf club. Cars are allowed on part of the beach. You can either walk across the golf course to the east of the dunes **F** or follow the beach southwards towards Parrog. At low tide, if the river is not in flood, you can wade across to the Boat Club quay, but be sure to test the depth of water first. If in doubt follow the north shore of the estuary towards the Iron Bridge.

On the upstream side of the Iron Bridge you will see stepping stones, which may be medieval. Close to the road there is a plaque on a stone plinth, erected by the National Park Authority and the Dyfed Wildlife Trust to help visitors identify some of the bird species that frequent the estuary in winter. Newport **6** is not actually on the coastal footpath, but Parrog is. To reach Parrog simply continue along the footpath for about half a mile (1 km), now heading westwards along the south shore of the estuary. There is a large free car park, with shops, café and toilet facilities.

Geology

The Pembrokeshire coastline is justly famous for its magnificent cliff scenery and for its immense variety of coastal habitats. Why is there such a range of coastal types within what is geographically a very small area?

Pembrokeshire rocks belong for the most part to the Palaeozoic Era and all of them are over 300 million years old. The oldest rocks are Precambrian, and are more than 1,000 million years old. Broadly, Pembrokeshire can be divided into two structural regions. In the 'northern geological province' the rocks are of Lower Palaeozoic and Precambrian age; many are made of sea-floor sediments, although there are also igneous rocks. All these rocks were laid down before the great Caledonian mountain-building episode which culminated about 400 million years ago, creating a gigantic mountain range along the contact of the two colliding supercontinents of North America and Eurasia. The great folds (anticlines and synclines) created during this episode are responsible for the south-west to north-east 'grain' of the country in North Pembrokeshire, and

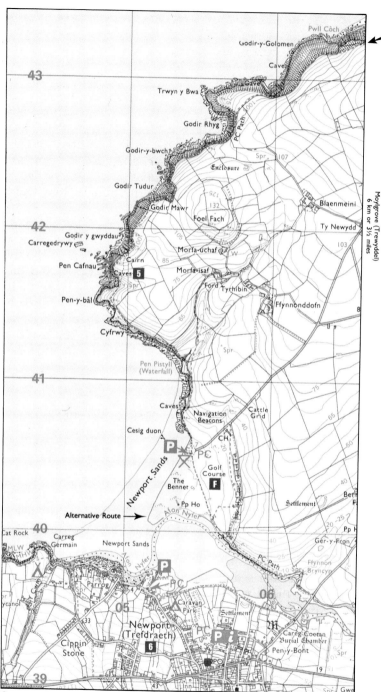

Pwll Côch
Godir-y-Golomen
Caves
Trwyn y Bwa
Caves
Godir Rhyg
PC Path
Godir-y-bwch
Enclosure
Spr
107
Godir Tudur
126
Blaenmeini
Godir Mawr
132
Ty Newydd
Foel Fach
Godir y gwyddau
Morfa-uchaf
103
Carregedrywy
W
Cairn
85
Pen Cafnau
Morfa-isaf
Caves **5**
Spr
Ford Tyrhibin
Pen-y-bâl
Ffynnonddofn
Cyfrwy
65
Pen Pistyll
(Waterfall)
Spr
75
Caves
Navigation
Beacons
Cattle
Grid
65
Cesig duon
CH
P
PC
Golf
Course
Newport Sands
The
Benner
F
Settlement
Ber
Pp Ho
Afon Nyfer
Alternative Route →
Ger-y-Fron
Cat Rock
Carreg
Pp H
MLW
Germain
Newport Sands
Flynnon
Bryncyn
PC Path
06
Parrog
P
PC
ycanol
05
Caravan
Park
Settlement
Cippin
Newport
(Trefdraeth)
PC
Careg Coetan
Burial Chamber
Stone
6
P **i**
Pen-y-Bont
Spr
PC
19
Inn
39
43
Gwe

Contours are given in metres
The vertical interval is 5m

Moylgrove (Trewyddel)
6 km or 3½ miles

33

around the coast the spectacular cliffs provide opportunities to examine 'slices' through these structures, with folds, faults, shattered belts and a whole host of other geological features beautifully revealed.

In North Pembrokeshire, too, the details of the coast are not due simply to the work of the sea. During the Ice Age the work of frost, glacier ice and glacial meltwater led to the creation of many spectacular 'fossil' features that clearly have nothing to do with present-day conditions. Elsewhere, ancient river valleys affect the appearance of the coastline, as at St Dogmaels, Newport and Newgale. In other places the work of wind is apparent, as at Whitesands, Poppit and Newport, where size-able dune systems have developed in conjunction with sandy beaches.

In South Pembrokeshire the rocks are younger, all of them belonging to the Upper Palaeozoic Era. Those most commonly encountered are the red sandstones and marls of the Old Red Sandstone formation, the grey and white soluble rocks of the Carboniferous Limestone formation, and the Coal Measures of the Pembrokeshire coalfield. The great majority are sedimentary, but some igneous rocks are to be found along the southern shore of St Bride's Bay. To the south of Newgale the folds and faults were created during another episode of mountain-building called the 'Armorican' or 'Hercynian' Orogeny, which occurred immediately after the deposition of the Coal Measures. This time the grain or trend of the structure is almost east–west.

The great sweep of St Bride's Bay is the result of coastal erosion from the west of the soft rocks of the coalfield, between the hard, resistant igneous promontories tipped by Ramsey Island in the north and Skomer Island in the south. The promontory of Pen Caer owes its survival to the resistance of hard igneous rocks. The waterway of Milford Haven owes its origin to river erosion along a series of faults and outcrops of Carboniferous Limestone, with the river valley later flooded by the sea. Saundersfoot Bay owes its origin to the marine erosion of soft Coal Measures rocks along the axis of a broad syncline. And if you look at the coastline in detail, time and again you will see the influence of geology or structure. Almost all of the headlands between Strumble Head and St David's Head coincide with outcrops of hard igneous rocks, while almost all of the bays coincide with outcrops of softer shale or mudstone. On the south shore of Milford Haven, the embayments of Angle

Bay and the Pembroke River coincide exactly with outcrops of easily eroded limestone, whereas the narrow bay entrances have been formed through breaches of a rampart of hard Old Red Sandstone. On the magnificent Carboniferous Limestone coasts of the Castlemartin Peninsula, narrow inlets coincide with faults and bands of broken rock or 'gash breccia'; headlands often coincide with outcrops of particularly massive limestone beds.

Marine erosion of soft shales at the base of the cliffs at Cwm-yr-Eglwys.

2 Newport (Parrog) to Goodwick (Harbour Heights)

via Cwm-yr-Eglwys and Fishguard
12½ miles (20 km)

This section of the route commences at Parrog, about half a mile (1 km) from the centre of Newport **6** and reached via Parrog Road. Newport itself is well served by a regular bus service between Fishguard and Cardigan. There are four inns in the town as well as a number of cafés, tea rooms and guest-houses. The National Park Information Centre is situated opposite the entrance of the Long Street car park. The national trail between Newport and Fishguard is well marked and should present no major problems.

The Parrog is Newport's old port. Before the silting of the estuary in the late 1800s, slates, herrings, woollen fabrics and other local products were exported, and culm, limestone, wine, fruit and other luxury items were imported. There was ship-building and ship-repairing too. Cwm is a small beach at the western end of the Parrog, used as the focal point for Newport's annual summer regatta.

The old port of Parrog, Newport, with the volcanic peak of Carn Ingli in the distance.

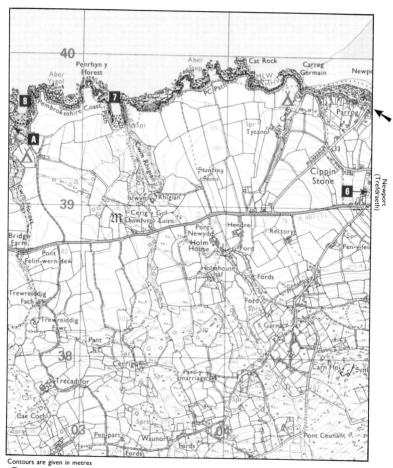

Contours are given in metres
The vertical interval is 5m

The bay to the west of Cat Rock, like the other bays between Newport and Cwm-yr-Eglwys, has been used for the quarrying of shale slabs locally referred to as slate. The 'sea quarries' belonged for the most part to the Llwyngwair Estate. The coast here is on an intimate scale, quite unlike that between St Dogmaels and Newport. Heading west from Parrog you reach Aberrhigian **7**, an idyllic little cove, totally unspoilt. Aberfforest **8** is very similar, with the cove occupying the seaward end of a valley. This is a popular little beach, with some sand exposed at low tide. There are reasonable conditions for launching small boats. The footbridge **A** was destroyed in a recent flood, so be prepared to get your feet wet when crossing the stream. Detour upstream if the river is in flood.

Cwm-yr-Eglwys **9** (the Valley of the Church) is one of North Pembrokeshire's favourite beauty spots. The small settlement nestles at the eastern end of the deep valley of Cwm Dewi, well sheltered from the prevailing westerly winds. This shelter has allowed the growth of trees and shrubs of almost Mediterranean luxuriance. There is a good sandy beach, a slipway for launching boats, toilets and a small car park. The focal point of the settlement is the ruined church of St Brynach, which at one time was well inland and large enough to hold a congregation of 300.

There are two alternatives at this point: either carry on round Dinas Island to Dinas Head, or follow the valley path **B** to Pwllgwaelod **10**. In the dense, moist woodland you should see many small birds, including garden warblers, chiffchaffs, willow warblers, whitethroats and blackcaps. Where the woodland gives way to more open conditions, look out for the pearl-bordered fritillary among the butterflies, and also the day-flying scarlet tiger moth. Frogs, adders and grass snakes are common on the edge of the boggy land. Throughout August listen for the sound of bush crickets during the late afternoon and early evening.

The path out to Dinas Head climbs through patches of scrub and woodland, which thrive on the lee side of the headland. Needle Rock is a stack close enough to the trail to provide excellent views of nesting seabirds: herring gulls, razorbills, guillemots and shags. Ravens, jackdaws, fulmars and other gulls also nest on the mainland cliffs hereabouts. Beyond it, the long bevelled slope, terminated by sheer cliffs at the coastline proper, is reminiscent of the north-facing cliffs of Traeth Cell-Howel, east of Morfa Head. The path can be slippery here **C**. Pen y Fan is the highest point on the headland, at 466 feet (142 metres), with glorious views in all directions. Look out for grey seals down below, and out to sea you may be lucky enough to see porpoises (with triangular dorsal fins) or dolphins (with beak-like snouts and sickle-shaped dorsal fins). You may also see peregrine falcons, and gannets diving for fish offshore.

Pwllgwaelod **10**, exposed to the westerly winds, provides a striking contrast to the lush, calm environment of Cwm-yr-Eglwys. It is a popular beach none the less, with firm, golden sand, a large car park, toilet facilities, a ruined lime kiln, and pub, café and restaurant. The next stretch of coast is fascinating, with dark shale cliffs and abundant creeks, offshore stacks and little beaches down below. Pwll Gwylog is a delightful little cove, with easy access to the beach.

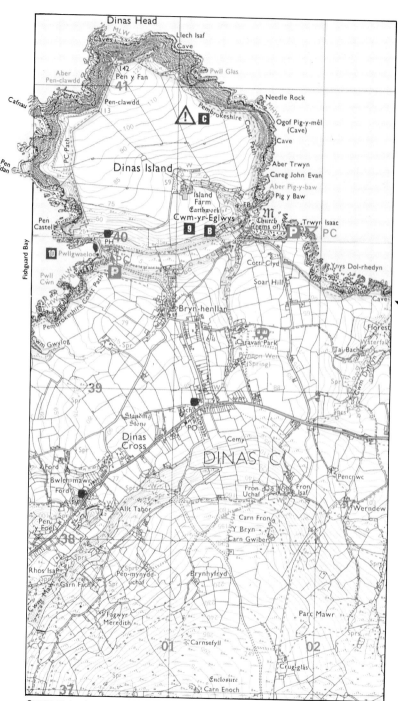

Contours are given in metres
The vertical interval is 5m

Hescwm (Aber Bach) **11** is a well-kept secret. The inlet is very well sheltered by the offshore stacks to the west. There is good bathing, although the beach is pebbly and rough. Access from the road is not easy; there is room for only a couple of cars on the verge near the entrance to Hescwm Mill. The path heads away from the beach for a while before swinging westwards again **D**. Look out for the fingerposts on the western side.

Penrhyn still has many traces of a First World War coastal defence installation. Now the site has been transformed into a well-planned caravan park. Needle Rock (another one!) is a spectacular stack with an arch punctured through its base, best viewed by scrambling down the slope below the Coast Path. Nesting bird species here, and on the cliffs adjacent to the stack, include fulmars, gulls, razorbills, guillemots and cormorants.

Continuing westwards you approach the sheltered waters of Fishguard Harbour and its 'three towns'. On Castle Point you

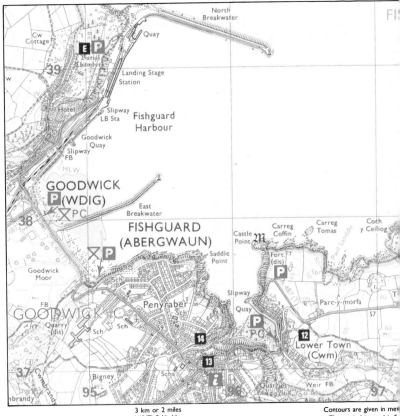

3 km or 2 miles
A40(T) Schleddau

Contours are given in met
The vertical interval is 5

come across the ruins of Fishguard Fort, built in 1781 to defend the community against privateers. Lower Town (Cwm) **12** is built around the drowned western end of Cwm Gwaun, Pembrokeshire's largest and most spectacular sub-glacial meltwater channel. Cwm was Fishguard's earliest settlement, earning its living from herring fishing, shipbuilding and coastal trading. From the old bridge you can either follow the main road up into the modern town of Fishguard **13**, or keep to the coast. Beyond the boat park you can follow a tarmac path towards The Slade **14**, or else (at low tide) walk along the beach. From The Slade there are a number of good paths to choose from, all following the slope along the western side of the Lower Town harbour. After passing Lampit Beach, follow the Marine Walk all the way to the picnic area and car park overlooking Goodwick (Parrog) beach. The Parrog car park is a convenient stop or start point close to garages and accommodation.

A CIRCULAR WALK AROUND DINAS HEAD

2½ miles (4.2 km)

Start at Pwllgwaelod **10** and follow the path in a clockwise direction; the steep slope to the east of Dinas Head is easier to descend than to ascend if the weather is wet! The route is almost all along the national trail, and is well marked. Start up the road above the Sailor's Safety Inn and turn off at the steep bend. Then follow the footpath to the summit at Pen y Fan. Descend towards Needle Rock and follow the path through the scrub woodland to Cwm-yr-Eglwys **9**. Explore the little settlement with its ruined church and massive sea defences. Then go through the car park and caravan site, heading westwards along Cwm Dewi, and back to the start. Parts of this path, especially at the eastern end of the valley, can be very muddy. This is an easy walk for an afternoon, but you need to be fit enough to climb to the Dinas Island summit at 466 feet (142 metres). There is an excellent natural history guide published by the Dyfed Wildlife Trust.

You can also start this walk at Cwm-yr-Eglwys **9**. However, there is less car parking space than at Pwllgwaelod.

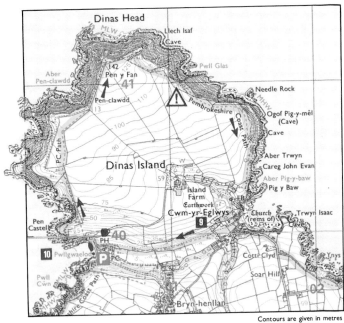

Contours are given in metres
The vertical interval is 5m

Goodwick is a large settlement clinging to a steep hillside. It owes its origins to the arrival of the railway and the creation of the port of Fishguard in Victorian times. From the centre of Goodwick climb up New Hill, which takes you past the Presbyterian Methodist chapel, and on above Fishguard Bay Hotel to Harbour Village. Enjoy the fine views across the harbour. Car parking (free) is at the northern end of Harbour Village, but there are no other facilities here at the end of the road **E**.

The 'three towns'

Fishguard (Abergwaun) is really made up of three quite distinct communities, Lower Town (occupying the mouth of the Gwaun Valley), the modern town of Fishguard (on the higher ground to the west), and Goodwick (occupying a steep hillside above Goodwick Moor and close to the modern port).

Lower Town (or 'Cwm' as it is locally known) is the archetypal fishing village, with houses clustered close to the waterfront mainly on the eastern flank of the old harbour. The settlement survived for centuries as a small trading centre with a substantial herring fishery. There was a local shipbuilding industry, and cargoes of limestone, coal, fabrics and foodstuffs came in to balance the exports of salted herrings, woollen cloth, oats and barley. Gradually, in the late 19th century, both fishing and coastal trading declined; today the harbour is full of pleasure craft. This is one of the prettiest coastal settlements in Wales; not surprisingly, it was chosen for the film version of Dylan Thomas's *Under Milk Wood*.

The modern town was but a cluster of cottages until the early 1800s, but gradually it expanded to become the main shopping centre of North Pembrokeshire. The Market Square is the centre of affairs, with the Town Hall and the Royal Oak inn, where the surrender documents were signed following the last invasion of Britain in 1797. A great deal of modern housing has now spread out along the undulating plateau surface to the north and west of the original town centre.

Fishguard Harbour was constructed in the early years of this century as a transatlantic passenger port, connected by rail with South Wales and London. The difficult site beneath east-facing cliffs was transformed by blasting. Two million tonnes of rock were removed, most of it built into the impressive 2,000-foot-long (610-metre) North Breakwater. The quarry floor was then used for the railway terminus, passenger station, storage sheds

The old fort near Lower Town, Fishguard.

and quayside equipment. The work continued until 1908, when the first passenger service was inaugurated. For six years (until the outbreak of the First World War) there was hectic activity, with ships of the Cunard, Blue Funnel and Booth lines all using the harbour for the Irish and transatlantic passenger services. Fishguard briefly threatened Liverpool as a transatlantic port, but the harbour lacked an industrial hinterland and could generate little economic activity locally, so its fall was as rapid as its rise. The building of the East Breakwater in 1913, intended to improve facilities, caused rapid harbour silting instead and soon it became impossible for the larger liners to tie up at the quayside. After the war the transatlantic service was not revived, but the port has remained important for the Irish service, with Sealink vessels ferrying passengers, vehicles and container traffic between Fishguard and Rosslare.

Goodwick was a sleepy fishing village before the coming of the railway and the growth of the port. For many years it was, above all, a railway settlement, but many local people were employed in the port and in a local brickworks. The latter is now closed. Above the village is Harbour Village, built around 1906 to house railway and port workers. The most imposing building in Goodwick is the Fishguard Bay Hotel, overlooking the harbour. There is a pleasant sandy beach on the Parrog, and good shops and car parks. The village now makes its living as a popular holiday and boating centre, and as the service centre for the port.

3 Goodwick (Harbour Heights) to Trefin

around Strumble Head and past Abercastle
17½ miles (28.2 km)

The starting point **E** is about 2 miles (3 km) from the centre of Fishguard (well served by buses) or 1 mile (1½ km) by road from Fishguard railway station, which is actually the station serving the ferry port. There is a good regular train service and a regular daily town service bus between Fishguard Square and Harbour Village. On leaving the Harbour Heights car park you are back to a proper footpath. The coastal path is well maintained and easy to follow all the way to Trefin.

The path runs well inland at Pen Anglas, cutting off the peninsula which is famous for the columnar jointing similar to that of Fingal's Cave. A little way past the headland you re-enter the National Park. From the summit of Carnfathach **15** you will see typical Pen Caer scenery. Inland lies the bleak expanse of Ciliau Moor, with the volcanic crag of Garnwnda beyond,

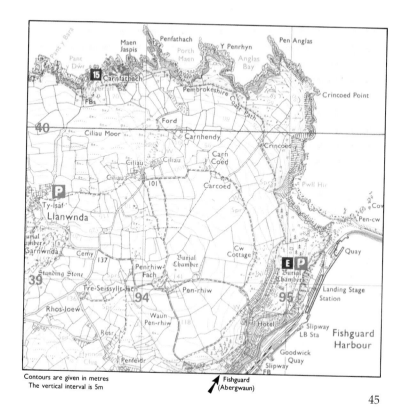

Contours are given in metres
The vertical interval is 5m

Fishguard
(Abergwaun)

45

smoothed during the Ice Age, like other neighbouring crags. Note the small rough fields, the stone walls, and the wind-blasted trees. Here and there in this harsh but beautiful environment you can see little clusters of settlement. The hamlet of Llanwnda is the main centre – half a dozen houses, an ancient green and a Celtic-style bellcote church restored in 1870.

At Cwm Felin you come unexpectedly across a most attractive and well-wooded little valley. A stream tumbles down to the shore under a canopy of lush woodland, and suddenly you hear woodland birds again. There is good shelter here in inclement weather – and it is the shelter from westerly winds that enables the deciduous trees to survive and even thrive. A well-marked footpath **A** runs inland from Cwm Felin to Llanwnda, where there is some car parking space.

Carreg Goffa **16** and Carregwastad Point are the scene of the last invasion of Britain, if this is not too grand a term for it, which took place on 22nd February 1797. The simple memorial stone on Carreg Goffa **16** was erected in 1897 to commemorate the landing of Colonel Tate and his 'invasion force' of 1,200 men. You can explore the peninsula before returning to the Coast Path.

The memorial stone at Carreg Goffa, erected to commemorate the 'Last Invasion of Britain' in 1797.

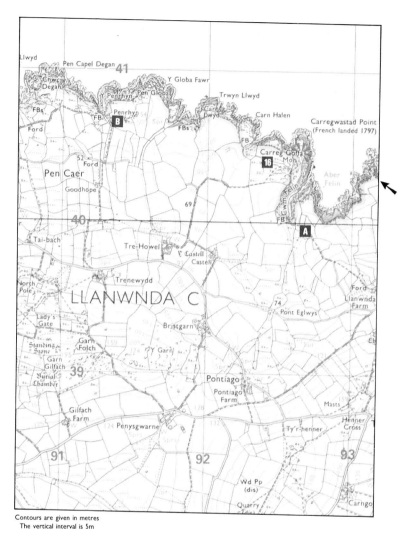

Contours are given in metres
The vertical interval is 5m

To the west of Pen Globa the path passes through an area of bluish-green dolerite outcrops, springy turf and gorse bushes. Abundant lichens and spring flowers make this a most colourful and fascinating stretch of the path. Penrhyn is an idyllic spot, with a lonely cottage located adjacent to the footpath. The pretty, whitewashed building sits on a grassy bank that runs down to a narrow creek. There are three possible routes here **B**. One runs southwards to Goodhope and Trenewydd; a second follows the track westwards to Tresinwen; and the third, on the clifftop, is the national trail.

47

Strumble Head **17** is a glorious, wild stretch of coast, savagely impressive during storm conditions and overlooked by the coastguard lookout building. Because of its easy access by road, it is also popular with naturalists. The restored Ministry of Defence building close to the car park provides birdwatchers with some shelter. This is an immensely popular spot among 'twitchers' who wish to observe the spring and autumn bird migrations at close quarters. Below the observation post there are some classic exposures of pillow lavas. The pillow-shaped masses are the result of the very rapid cooling of volcanic lavas extruded on to the sea floor during submarine eruptions about 450 million years ago. A little further to the west the lighthouse on the island of Ynys Meicel is sometimes accessible via a small footbridge. It is not manned, and is therefore not normally open to the public.

The trail follows a beautiful stretch of coast between Carreg Onnen Bay and Pen Brush, about 1¼ miles (2 km) away, weaving in and out of a range of little hillocks of volcanic rock, all rounded and smoothed by ice action. Pwll Arian (loosely translated, Silver Cove or Treasure Cove) is a delightful spot where a small valley runs down to the sea. Banks of springy turf, reed beds and copses of bushes make this an ideal location for a picnic. As you walk south-eastwards from Pen Brush there is shelter in old Ministry of Defence buildings both above and below the footpath. Porth Maenmelyn is a wild little cove. Dinas Mawr is an Iron Age promontory fort defended by a double embankment. Keep an eye open for choughs hereabouts, and also for breeding seals in the late autumn. Pwllderi Youth Hostel is nearby.

Pwll Deri **18** is one of Pembrokeshire's favourite beauty spots, eroded by the sea along soft shales and bounded to the north by a great mass of dolerites and other hard volcanic rocks. These igneous rocks have been resistant to marine erosion, and remain as wave-swept offshore islands, stacks and skerries, while the softer sedimentary rocks have been eroded away. On its south side the bay is bordered by the great rampart of cliffs running for 1¼ miles (2 km) south-westwards towards Penbwchdy. In places these cliffs are over 450 feet (137 metres) high, providing Pwllderi Youth Hostel (opened in 1957) with the most exposed and spectacular site of all the hostels in Pembrokeshire. After climbing up to the road **C**, pass the memorial stone and small car parking area before rejoining the footpath proper to head south-west towards Carn Ogof.

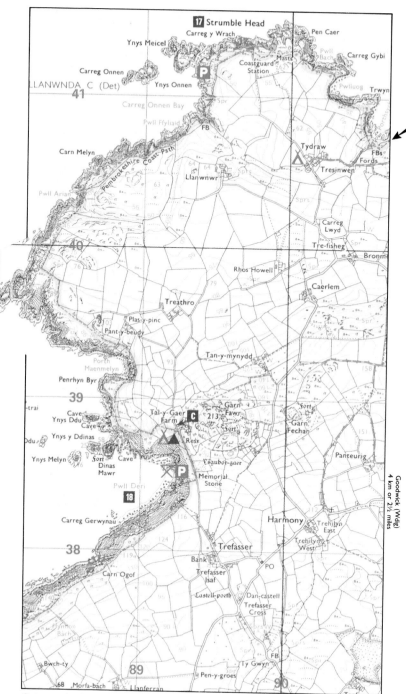

Contours are given in metres
The vertical interval is 5m

49

The treeless, windswept landscape of Pencaer, from the summit of Garn Fawr.

rumble Head lighthouse is in the distance.

If you look inland from Penbwchdy towards St Nicholas, you can see a strange hilltop structure on the skyline. This is 'Green One', the civil aircraft homing beacon used by transatlantic traffic. From the footpath at Penbwchdy, looking westwards towards the tip of the peninsula, you can also see a circular, dry stone structure.

Now continue to Pwllcrochan, an attractive small bay cut into contorted and broken soft sedimentary rocks, with some sand exposed at low tide. Access is difficult, but it is possible to scramble down to the beach near stile 335. Further south, Aber Bach is a pretty bay with a massive storm beach that has impounded a small stream in the valley. Notice the little ruined boathouse.

Aber Mawr **19** has a wide sandy beach backed by an impressive storm beach of pebbles. Access is good, and there is reasonable parking for 15–20 cars on the roadside verge. Aber Mawr is probably the most important Ice Age site in Pembrokeshire. The cliffs of unconsolidated sediments at the north end of the bay reveal a sequence of deposits from the last glacial episode, while the organic deposits on the floor of the valley behind the storm beach span the last 14,000 years or so. The submerged forest is occasionally exposed through the sandy beach following winter storms. The old roadway that once connected the two sides of the bay has gradually been eroded away, because the coast has retreated inland by about 130 feet (40 metres). Descend to the storm beach and continue to the southern end of the bay, where you again rejoin the footpath.

In the lee of Penmorfa the cliffs are extremely well protected from the prevailing westerlies and south-westerlies. Note that the cliff profiles are much gentler, affording easy access to the sea in many places. In contrast, the west-facing cliffs across the bay are steep and constantly battered by storm waves. On the peninsula, Castell-coch is an Iron Age promontory fort with double embankments and ditches, and a zigzag central entrance designed to resist direct attack. There are lovely views from the outer part of Trwyn Llwynog peninsula. Continue to Aber Mochyn ('the bay of the pig'). Be careful of clifftop instability here – you will see much evidence of subsidence, rockfalls and rotational slips in the cliff face **D**.

The footpath is dangerous on the western side of the little cove of Pwllstrodur **E**. Be careful in wet weather as this section could slide away at any time.

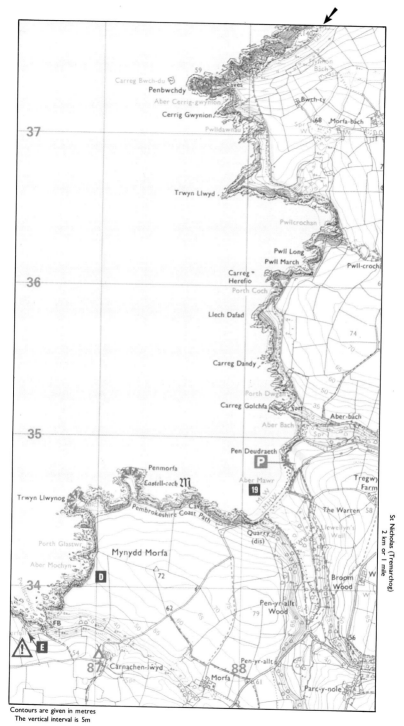

Contours are given in metres
The vertical interval is 5m

You soon see a most impressive field wall, labelled by the weary builder 'The Great Wall of China'. Then, a further half-mile to the west, you come upon Abercastle. This is a delightful creek – one of the multitude of little harbours on the Pembrokeshire coast used by trading vessels until well into the present century. There is a cluster of houses and cottages around the head of the inlet, and a number of other typical features – an old granary (roofless and derelict), two fine bollards (made of old cannons embedded in the turf), a lime kiln and the remains of a lime-burner's cottage.

Carreg Sampson cromlech (burial chamber) **20** can be reached via stiles adjacent to the trail. The capstone is over 16 feet (5 metres) long and almost 10 feet (3 metres) wide, resting on three of the six uprights. The burial chamber was built about 5,000 years ago; it was probably used for at least 100 different burials by the Neolithic tribe in whose territory it lay.

Further west, Pen Castell-coch is a delightful peninsula, projecting far out from the coast and connected to the mainland by a narrow neck. It is a splendid spot for a picnic – springy turf, flowers in spring, skylarks and seabirds, and wonderful coastal

1 km or ½ mile
Llanrhian

Contours are given in metres
The vertical interval is 5m

views to the south-west. There is rapid coastal erosion beyond the peninsula. Note the rock pinnacles, rockfalls, fault scarps and cliff-face slumps. To the south, Pwll Llong is a small bay contained by high cliffs and accessible via a steep path, but the beach is rocky and pebbly. Many fulmars nest hereabouts. There is footpath access to Trefin and the youth hostel from the national trail just to the east of Trwyn Llwyd **F**.

Aber Draw (Aber Felin) is the beach for Trefin **21**. It is too rocky and exposed ever to have played much part in coastal trading, but there is a sandy beach at low water. The ruined Melin Trefin was one of the multitude of little corn mills that served the farming community in the last century. You can also reach Trefin by bearing left up the hill when you get to the tarmac road. It is the largest of the coastal villages between St David's and Goodwick. One of the early palaces of the Bishop of St David's was built here, but is now lost without trace. Although just off the national trail, Trefin is a good point for stopping or starting a walk, being served by a youth hostel, an inn and a village store. There is also a regular daily bus service between St David's and Fishguard.

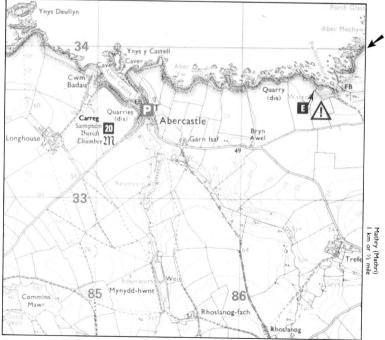

Contours are given in metres
The vertical interval is 5m

55

The Celts and their forts

The Celtic immigrant tribes who moved into Pembrokeshire about 2,600 years ago made a more dramatic and lasting impact upon the landscape than any of their predecessors. They were more ferocious, more organised, and more practised in the arts of war and peace than the Bronze Age settlers already in residence, and as the centuries passed they tamed large parts of the Pembrokeshire wilderness by clearing the forest, building villages and fortifications, and introducing many new agricultural practices. They sowed and harvested new crops, kept domesticated animals, and enclosed fields and paddocks with dry stone walls. They also rode horses, which made them fearsome warriors, and they had armour and weapons far in advance of anything used by the Bronze Age people.

It is often said that whereas the Bronze Age people practised the arts of peace, the Iron Age invaders practised the arts of war. Things were certainly not that simple, but such was the scale of the immigration into western Britain that inter-tribal and even inter-family feuding must have become a way of life, as groups of all sizes jostled for the best land, the best water supplies, and the best-defended sites.

The Iron Age hill fort or promontory fort is the most striking of all the prehistoric features to be found in Wales, and in Pembrokeshire such forts are particularly numerous. Earth ramparts and ditches appear with almost predictable regularity on hill summits, river valley spurs, and – of most interest to those walking the national trial – on coastal promontories all the way around the coast. Almost every self-respecting headland has its promontory fort, and the features of earth and stone provide an insight into the evolution of defensive strategies as the Iron Age ran its course. The earliest forts were protected only by single-curved banks and ditches, but by 100 BC double, triple and even quadruple embankments and ditches were common, with complicated entrance passages and assorted devices designed to repel boarders. Many embankments were faced with stone; sometimes these were over 15 feet (4.5 metres) high, and sometimes they bristled with pointed stakes. No doubt the defenders knew all about arrows, spears, boulders and boiling water too. Sometimes the enclosed areas were very small, and were used only as last-ditch defensive positions (which is where the phrase probably comes from); but other fortified sites enclosed areas of land large enough to enable a family group and its animals to sit out a prolonged siege.

Some of the promontory forts contain traces of Iron Age hut circles (as on St David's Head), and here and there you can see traces of Iron Age field boundaries. The largest of all the coastal defended sites is the Deer Park at Martin's Haven, but those who feel like a short detour from the trail can climb Garn Fawr (close to Pwll Deri) or Carn Ingli (close to Newport) for a glimpse of a genuine hill summit settlement with all its trappings.

The Neolithic cromlech or burial chamber of Carreg Sampson, near Abercastle, with Pencaer in the background.

4 Trefin to Whitesands Bay

via Porth-gain and Abereiddi
11¼ miles (18 km)

Starting from Trefin, follow the road westwards to Aber Draw beach and climb up the hill on the far side of the valley. Where signposted, turn right, off the road.

The trail is difficult to find in this area **A**. Simply follow the farm track westwards across the fields. Note the volcanic boulders conveniently collected by generations of farmers from the fields. After passing the waterfall in Pwll Crochan Bay, stick to the footpath; small ploughed fields intervene between the path and the coastline. After making contact with the coast again, you come to a choice of routes **B**. Either take the shortcut to Porth-gain **22** or follow the coast via Trwyn Elen. Porth-gain **22** is a fascinating place, heavy with the atmosphere of Pembrokeshire's short-lived Industrial Revolution. The little harbour was used in the period 1837–1931 for the export of roadstone, slates and bricks. Note the remains of the old brickworks and the massive bins that held the crushed stone.

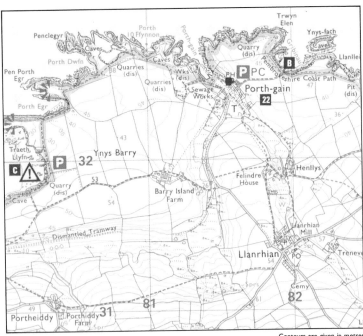

Contours are given in metres
The vertical interval is 5m

Walk out along the western edge of the harbour and climb the steps near the old pilot house. On the cliff tops look for traces of Pentop quarrymen's row, the slate/shale quarry and tramway cutting, trackbeds galore, dust and crushed stone, the remains of the stone-crushing plant, the old weighbridge, water tank and engine shed, spoil tips of slate rubble, and the small fields used by the eight horses that pulled the tramway trucks prior to 1909. Out towards Penclegyr you will see the vast dolerite quarry with two levels and the cable-worked incline (to the bottom level), the railway cutting (to the upper level), the winding house and smithy remains, connected by 'the Jerusalem Road' to the yard, with loops and loco shed further east. There is a rutted track to Traeth Llyfn and there may well have been a short-lived tramway here around 1880, connecting the Penclegyr stone quarry with Abereiddi.

Traeth Llyfn is an attractive sandy beach backed by dark shale cliffs. It is somewhat claustrophobic, but the sand is good and the bathing safe. Beware of dangerous cliffs and being cut off by a rising tide when you are on the left-hand side of the beach **C**. Access is via a steep path. There is an approach for vehicles through Barry Island Farm to a car park near the cliff top.

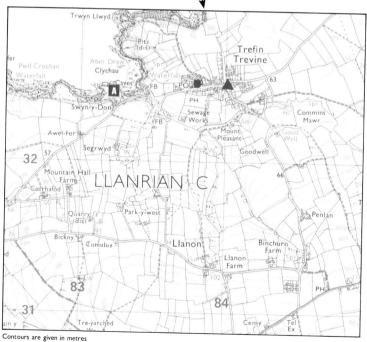

Contours are given in metres
The vertical interval is 5m

Further to the west, you can enjoy the lovely views from the summit of Carn Lŵyd, a crag of the Ordovician volcanic rock which runs out to the headland of Trwyncastell. The stone tower on the headland may be an 18th century 'pharos' tower rather than a harbour entrance marker.

Abereiddi Slate Quarry **23**, operational from about 1830 to 1904, produced slate of poor quality. Dressed slates were taken in horse-drawn trucks along the tramway to a slate yard near Barry Island Farm, and thence to Porth-gain for shipment. Buildings still visible at Abereiddi Quarry include dressing sheds, the engine house (on the ledge above the flooded quarry called the Blue Lagoon), the quarrymen's row, the round powder store, and the buttressed quarry manager's house. The bay is popular with visitors because the free car park gives direct access to the black sandy beach. The cluster of simple cottages, lime kiln and industrial relics combine to make this a favourite spot with artists. There are no facilities apart from a toilet block and an occasional ice-cream van.

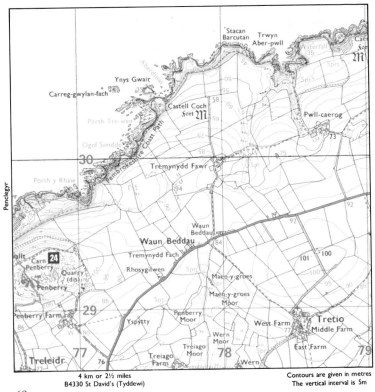

4 km or 2½ miles
B4330 St David's (Tyddewi)

Contours are given in metres
The vertical interval is 5m

From Abereiddi follow the road southwards until a fingerpost directs you back to the Coast Path. Soon you come to Caerau, a most impressive complex of three Iron Age forts, with well-preserved ditches, embankments and stone-faced ramparts. After a mile or so the Iron Age theme continues when you encounter yet another Castell Coch, set in the midst of wild and chaotic cliff scenery, with a double ditch and embankment across the headland.

From Porth y Rhaw onwards you are walking on hard igneous rocks. Note the contrast in appearance between the cliffs to the west and the soft crumbly cliffs to the north-east. Above Penclegyr the path climbs up quite steeply on the flank of Carn Penberry (Penbiri) **24**. This was an island in Pliocene times, when the gently undulating platform of the St David's peninsula was being fashioned by wave action. Near the point

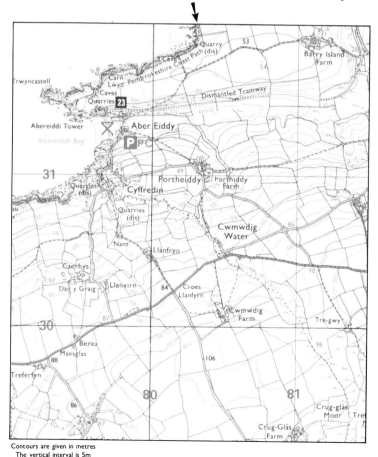

Contours are given in metres
The vertical interval is 5m

where the path splits **D** you will see a veritable rock garden with gorse and many other flowering species at their best in early summer. This is reputed to be the spot where Ffos y Mynach (the Monk's Dyke) reaches the coast.

Must of the coast to the west of Penberry is in the ownership of the National Trust. It is worth protecting, with complicated geology, fine cliffs, the hill masses of Carnedd-Ileithr, Carn Perfedd and Carn Treliwyd to the south, and carpets of flowers in the early summer. From the footpath you will catch glimpses of the 'deserted village' of Maes-y-mynydd, complete with ruined buildings, stone-walled fields and other enclosures. The village is probably medieval, but may go back to the Iron Age.

After passing the inlet of Gesail-fawr and the peninsula of Penllechwen, the Coast Path is difficult to discern, but it matters not – you can wander about more or less at will, as this is still National Trust land. This is another fabulous stretch of coastline for wild flowers. The cliffs are extremely popular with climbers. As you wander south-westwards through this heathery rock garden, look across the valley towards the rocky hill of Carn

Contours are given in metres
The vertical interval is 5m

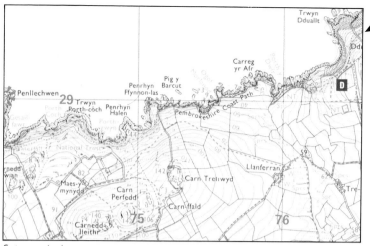

Contours are given in metres
The vertical interval is 5m

Llidi; there is hardly a trace of any man-made feature in the landscape, and you feel yourself transported back in time. But look carefully and you will see that on both sides of the valley there are signs of low and irregular Iron Age field boundaries.

As you approach the bleak peninsula of St David's Head, look out for Coetan Arthur **25**, a somewhat crude Neolithic burial chamber dating back to about 3,500 BC. A large flat capstone is supported at one end by a single vertical pillar and at the other end rests on the ground. Around the cromlech is a largely unaltered Ice Age landscape, with glaciated slabs and massive erratic boulders. But look closer, and you will see the hand of prehistoric man. Clawdd-y-Milwyr (the Warrior's Dyke) is a magnificent defensive line of two ramparts and three ditches almost at the tip of the peninsula. The main dry stone wall was originally 15 feet (4.5 metres) high. Within the defended area there are eight hut circles, all clearly visible.

Once you have rounded the peninsula, Porthmelgan is a pleasant sandy beach, easily accessible from Whitesands Bay. As a consequence there is very heavy use of this stretch of the path, resulting in severe erosion in places. The National Trust and the National Park Authority are taking remedial measures.

At Whitesands **26** there is a good car park (not free), shop, telephone and toilets. There is no inn and no accommodation, however, and the weary traveller will need to walk to the youth hostel on the south side of Carn Llidi (about half a mile from the beach) or to St David's, in order to find repose.

A CIRCULAR WALK TO ST DAVID'S HEAD AND CARN LLIDI
3½ miles (5.6 km)

Start and finish at Whitesands Bay car park **26**, where you will find a shop/café and toilets. This is an energetic half-day walk. Walk whichever way you like; I will describe the route anticlockwise. Walk up the road and take the second turning left. Climb to Upper Porthmawr and continue to the edge of the cultivated land. If you want to climb to the summit of Carn Llidi, turn left and climb to Highwinds before swinging east to the summit crags. Otherwise turn right and follow the path along the stone wall at the base of the steep slope. Swing northwards over the eastern shoulder of the hill and descend to the coast. Now you join the national trail, which is not well-defined, since walkers take their own route across open heathland south-westwards towards St David's Head. Take a look at Coetan Arthur burial chamber **25** and Clawdd-y-Milwyr defences and settlement site. Descend to Porthmelgan, climb up the other side of the valley and keep to the trail back to Whitesands.

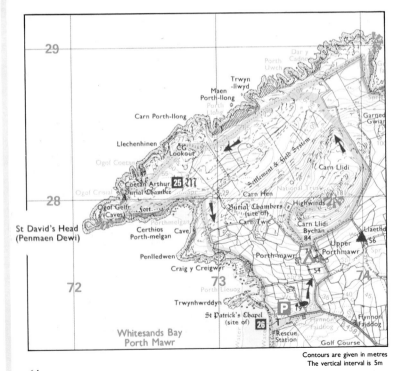

Contours are given in metres
The vertical interval is 5m

The peak of Carn Llidi, dominating the wild, rocky landscape inland of St David's Head.

The heyday of the little ports

In this peninsula the little ports and harbours were vital for the smooth operation of the local economy. Until the building of good roads, and until the arrival of the railway in the mid 19th century, Pembrokeshire's contacts with the outside world were almost all by sea. Just as the early immigrants arrived by sea, the western seaways in general, and the Celtic seaways in particular, kept trading and cultural contacts alive for well over 1,000 years. The Vikings, although they caused a certain amount of local trouble, heralded the dawn of an era of sea trading. They used larger and more seaworthy vessels than anything seen before around these coasts. The Normans and their followers further developed trading links, and these were maintained until the early part of the present century.

Because each small creek or inlet served its own small community there was little or no trading competition in the early centuries; every creek or cove with reasonable shelter became the base for small sailing vessels and even for shipbuilding operations. Lime kilns appeared all around the coastline, sometimes adjacent to quite exposed beaches where the landing of limestone and coal must have been hazardous, to say the least. Among the main shipbuilding centres were Newport, St Dogmaels, Solva, Dale and Angle. Fishguard, Pembroke, Haverfordwest and Tenby developed as sizeable trading centres and by 1600 there were many wealthy merchants. The main items of coastal trade were coal, corn, hides, raw wool and woollen cloth, timber and slate shipped out; and luxury goods, wine, fruit, spices, pitch and fine cloths shipped in. The growth of the herring fishery went hand-in-hand with the rise of Fishguard and Tenby, and in the sheltered waters of Milford Haven the oyster and cockle fishery was of great importance to Llangwm, Lawrenny and Angle.

In the 17th and 18th centuries smuggling and piracy became popular local activities, and some of the wealthy local gentry became, very mysteriously, even wealthier. The main cargoes in smuggled goods were wine, salt and tobacco, but gold, silver, spices, silks and other luxury goods appeared from time to time in the most unlikely places.

The scale of local trade was most impressive in the period 1550–1850. For example, in 1680 there were no less than 793 registered shipping movements in and out of Pembrokeshire ports, and goodness knows how many unregistered ones. In

A busy summer's day in Saundersfoot Harbour, which started life as a coal-exporting port.

the later part of this period, stone, slate and coal began to figure prominently in coastal trading, and ports such as Porth-gain, Newport, Lawrenny, Nolton and Saundersfoot began to specialise in the handling of mineral cargoes. But, as with general trading activities, the coming of the roads and railways opened up the interior of Pembrokeshire, and with the arrival of the traction engine and then the internal combustion engine it became impossible for the small trading vessels based in the small ports to compete. By the end of the First World War most of the sailing vessels and barges had been sold, or were laid up as rotting hulks. Now there are only the derelict stone quays, the bollards, the little warehouses and the coastal lime kilns to remind us of this fascinating episode in Pembrokeshire history.

5 Whitesands Bay to Solva

taking in Porth Clais and St Non's Bay
12¼ miles (19.8 km)

Whitesands Bay **26** can be reached quite easily from St David's. There is no public transport service, but if you take the road north-west from the cathedral car park you will reach the bay after a walk of 1½ miles (2.5 km). Then follow the Coast Path, which is so well marked all the way to Solva that instead of concentrating on finding your way you can relax and enjoy the cliff scenery, which is quite magnificent. As you walk take note of the excellent National Trust management work.

The bay (Porth Mawr) has one of Pembrokeshire's finest sandy beaches. The bathing is safe (especially in the middle and south of the beach) and there are good surfing and wind-surfing conditions. But beware of a dangerous undertow and currents near Trwynhwrddyn Headland; look out for the red flag. Lifesaving equipment is available, and lifeguards are on duty during the main holiday season.

Most of the rocks along this stretch of coast are of Cambrian age – they are predominantly greenish sandstones. But south of Ogofgolchfa there are exposures of the beautiful Cambrian basal conglomerate near the path. This strange rock looks like an ornamental concrete made for a rock garden, packed as it is with rounded cobbles and pebbles of purple, red and white quartzite, jasper and ash derived from the nearby Precambrian volcanic rocks. The conglomerate is about 570 million years old.

The stretch from Porthselau to St Justinian's is one of the easiest cliff walks on the trail. After rounding Point St John there are lovely views across the sound to Ramsey Island **27** (see partial map on page 70).

St Justinian's (Porthstinian) **28** is easily reached by road from St David's and there is reasonable car parking near the lifeboat station. The anchorage is very exposed, but it is used none the less by the Ramsey Island passenger boats, a few fishing boats and assorted pleasure craft. The lifeboat station was built in 1911–12. A little way to the south, Castell Heinif is one of the more impressive Iron Age forts, with a double embankment and a deeply excavated ditch. At the safe, deep and sheltered anchorage of Carn ar Wig note the old concrete quay and rusting winding-gear. This was the anchorage for the boats belonging to the Ramsey Island Farm.

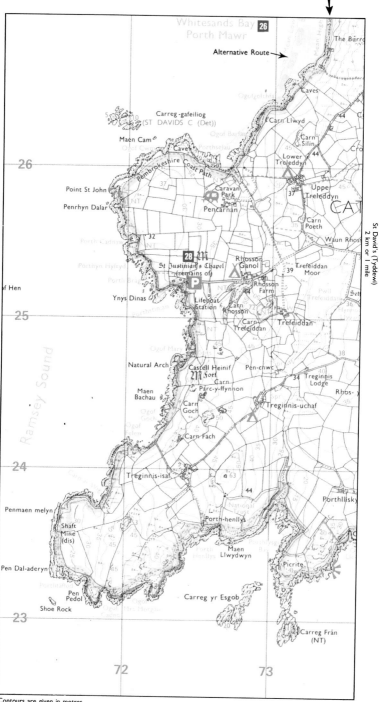

Contours are given in metres
The vertical interval is 5m

The Bitches are a series of fearsome rocks running out into the narrowest part of Ramsey Sound. The Great Bitch, closest to Ramsey, is split apart and also has a natural arch. From the mainland you can see (and hear!) the tide rushing through the Bitches; the tidal stream reaches a speed of 7 knots at times. This part of the Sound is a fearsome one for seafarers, and the Bitches have claimed many vessels.

Continuing southward past Penmaen melyn, look out for the huge glacial erratic boulder, 14 feet (4.25 metres) long and 8 feet (2.4 metres) high, one of the most impressive to be seen anywhere on the trail. A little further on, the Ramsey Sound copper mine **29** is a somewhat mysterious relic. Did it ever produce decent copper ore? Was copper produced here in the Bronze Age for combining with Cornish tin to make bronze? Or is this simply a speculative hole in the ground, of much later date, which never produced anything? The mine was certainly worked intermittently during the 19th century, and was referred to by the locals as 'Cuba'. Note the old shaft (fenced off), the piles of mine waste, and the remains of a crude building.

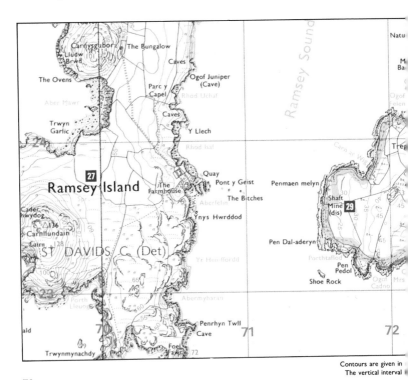

Contours are given in
The vertical interval

From Pen Dal-aderyn there are superb views of the cliff scenery on the south side of Ramsey Island **27**. Walking eastwards now, you come to Porthlysgi after about a mile (1½ km). The bay is named after Lysgi, a wicked Irish chieftain. This is not a good bathing beach; hardly any sand is exposed, even at low tide. Edible sea kale grows near the stream mouth. Close to the old track there are the ruins of the first St David's lifeboat station, used for housing the *Augusta*, which did sterling service between 1869 and 1885.

Porth Clais **30** has always been the harbour for the city of St David's, used by saints, disciples and pilgrims during the Age of the Saints, and by little trading vessels during the centuries that followed. The small breakwater may date from Norman times, but it was extensively restored in 1722. At the head of the creek you will see two stone quarries, four lime kilns (three of them very carefully restored) and the old trading quays. The car park is on the site of the old gasworks which provided town gas to the village-city until 1950. Although the inner part of the creek dries completely at low tide, Porth Clais still has a few fishing boats and is popular with the owners of pleasure craft.

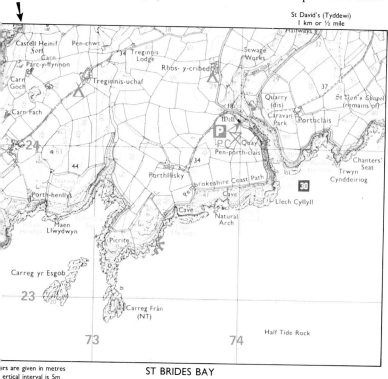

ST BRIDES BAY

St Non's Bay **31** is a place of peace, named after the mother of St David. The patron saint was born here during a great storm about AD 462, and the ruined chapel marks the spot. The holy well of St Non was a famous healing well, especially renowned for curing eye diseases. St Non's Retreat was built by the Passionist Fathers in 1929, and the present St Non's chapel was built (in the authentic early-Celtic style) in 1934, using stones from the ruins of nearby Whitewell Priory.

Caerfai Bay has a sheltered sandy beach, justifiably popular with visitors to St David's and easily reached by car. Some of the red and purple sandstone used for St David's Cathedral was taken from the quarries below the car park. There is good access to the beach if you are prepared to climb back up again afterwards! To the east, Penpleidiau is a magnificent Iron Age fort, with four defensive embankments and ditches. Caer Bwdy Bay is an attractive small bay, accessible from the main road at Pont Clegyr. Adjacent to the footpath you will see a massive and unusual square lime kiln and the remains of an old corn mill with millstones and some of the machinery still intact.

At Trelerw you can see a typical small Celtic settlement cluster. Hamlets like this were scattered all over the St David's peninsula; some of them probably date back to the Iron Age.

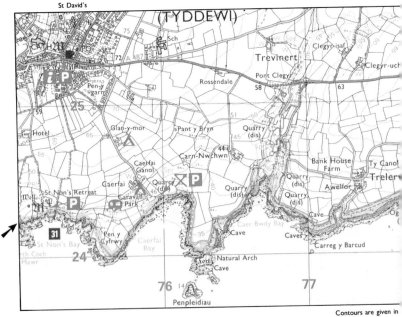

Contours are given in
The vertical interval

Porth y Rhaw is at the mouth of another meltwater channel and there are steep gradients on both sides of the valley **A**. At the head of the valley there were nine holy wells, much visited by the sick in the medieval period.

After a further half-mile or so the path swings northwards as you approach Solva **32**. Close to the village the path is not well marked, but you are unlikely to get lost; walk straight on into Upper Solva or descend to the quayside.

Solva Harbour is a ria – the drowned outer portion of a complex meltwater channel that extends right into the heart of the St David's peninsula. In the 1300s it was a small port and it developed as the main trading centre on the coasts of St Bride's Bay. In the 1770s the first Smalls lighthouse was conceived and built at Solva, and shipped out to the lethal Smalls rocks, 22 miles (35 km) offshore. Solva was the main lime-burning centre for the St David's peninsula, and in Victorian times there were 10 kilns in operation. The group of kilns on the flank of the Gribin **33**, near the car park, is worth examining. On the Gribin, notice the promontory fort at the tip of the peninsula and traces of a large settlement at its inland end.

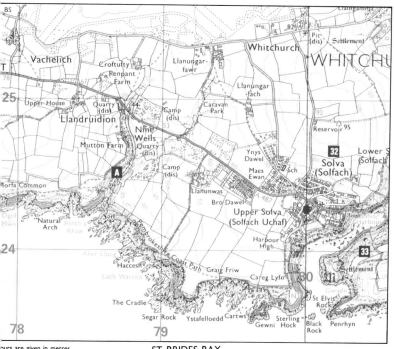

ST BRIDES BAY

St David and the Age of the Saints

The centuries that followed the departure of the Romans from Britain are generally referred to as the Dark Ages. But here in West Wales there was a thriving Christian community involved in a great flowering of civilisation. The 'Age of the Saints' spread across the western seaways to incorporate Ireland, the Isle of Man, North Wales, Pembrokeshire and Cornwall. There was a constant traffic in ideas, and the people of this western world were united by language, religion and art.

St David was one of the key figures of this period, although we must recognise that he was but one of many hundreds of devout and ascetic men who gave their lives to God as missionaries or monks in this far-flung corner of the Christian world. David was born at St Non's, baptised at Porth Clais, and educated near the little city that now bears his name. He spent most of his missionary life far away from his home area in other parts of the Celtic world, but in his old age returned to be revered as a great Christian leader. Monks and disciples travelled to his *llan* (monastic settlement) from other parts of Wales, from Brittany, Cornwall and Ireland. After his death in AD 588 his cult grew in strength; over 100 churches and monasteries were established in his name and pilgrims began to visit the little settlement in increasing numbers. Other sites of pilgrimage in the St David's peninsula included St Non's, Nine Wells, St Justinian's, and Porthmawr (Whitesands) – all having strong associations with the patron saint.

The cathedral of St David is, of course, the focal point of the little city, and is easily reached from the Coast Path. It nestles in the secluded valley of the River Alun, its tower just visible from the open coast. The present building is some way from the original monastic settlement and it is at least the fourth cathedral on this site; three earlier ones having been destroyed by the Vikings. The current structure was commenced in 1180, but it took several centuries of work under a succession of bishops to give it its present form. Adjacent to the cathedral itself are the buildings of St Mary's College and the remains of the magnificent Bishop's Palace, built by Bishop Gower in 1328–47.

6 Solva to Little Haven

passing Newgale, Nolton Haven and Broad Haven
12 miles (19.5 km)

Solva is well served by a daily bus service between St David's and Haverfordwest, and there are good shops, inns and guesthouses. There is also ample parking space at the head of the creek. Start this stretch from the village **32**, crossing the river from the car park and taking the footpath along the Gribin ridge **33**. Close to the seaward end of the ridge, descend to Gwadn **A**, cross the valley, and climb up to the Coast Path on the cliff top. The first part of this walk is well marked and relatively easy.

Dinas Fawr **34** is a lovely peninsula and well worth exploring. There are some traces of an Iron Age fort, but most of the embankments and pits at the neck of the peninsula are the remains of an ancient copper mine worked in Tudor times. Take a detour off the national trail; it is easy walking along the ridge to the peninsula tip. Enjoy the mass of wild flowers in the early summer. There are glorious views of the coast to east and west, and with luck you can watch gannets fishing in the bay.

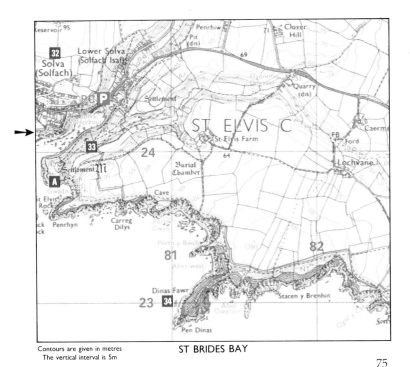

Contours are given in metres
The vertical interval is 5m

ST BRIDES BAY

The pebble beach at Newgale, formed by the storm waves that assault the coast

f St Bride's Bay.

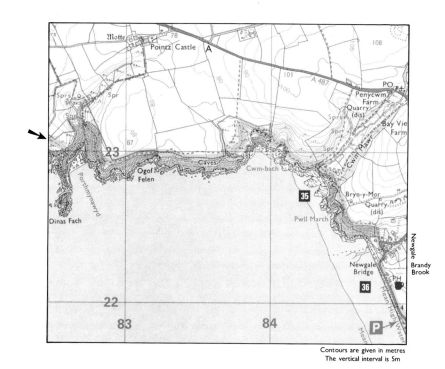

Contours are given in metres
The vertical interval is 5m

Dinas Fach, to the east, is a wild and jagged peninsula, with a spectacular blowhole close to its tip. In early summer, as you continue round the corner into Porthmynawyd, you are confronted by great sheets of blue vernal squill on the clifftop slope. This little valley is one of Pembrokeshire's surprises, with ferns, brambles, willow trees, sea buckthorn, flag irises and woodland birds. There is a small sandy beach, sometimes referred to as 'Pointz Castle Beach'.

Tucked into the north-eastern corner of St Bride's Bay, Penycwm beach **35** is easily accessible, with good footpaths from the hamlet on the main road. There are the remains of a small brickworks here, close to the cliff edge. The little pink cottage was that of the manager. A tramway ran up the valley to the main road. In this area you cannot escape the presence of RAF Brawdy, for Penycwm lies close to the end of one of the airfield runways. Do not be surprised by the sight (and sound) of low-flying jets.

Spectacular exposures of Cambrian sedimentary rocks (sandstones, conglomerates, shales, fault breccias, etc.) can be examined here at low tide. If you follow the beach southwards, be aware of the tide.

Newgale **36** is the most impressive sandy beach in Pembrokeshire, stretching for almost 2½ miles (4 km) towards Rickets Head. There is wonderful flat sand, and while Newgale is popular for bathing, you must watch out for a powerful undertow on a falling tide when there is a strong sea running. The surfing is splendid, especially out of the main holiday season, and the beach is becoming increasingly popular for sea fishing and sand yachting. Brandy Brook marks the western end of the Pembrokeshire Landsker – the invisible dividing line between the Welsh- and English-speaking parts of Pembrokeshire.

Follow the minor road, the pebble beach crest, or the sandy beach **B**. The valley side and slopes above the car park give you your first sight of Pembrokeshire's Coal Measures. Note the traces of colliery waste, and the ubiquitous lime kilns. There were 26 shafts hereabouts in the 1800s. When you pass the car park and beach café it is best to follow the road uphill and then return to the footpath proper when invited to do so by a fingerpost on your right.

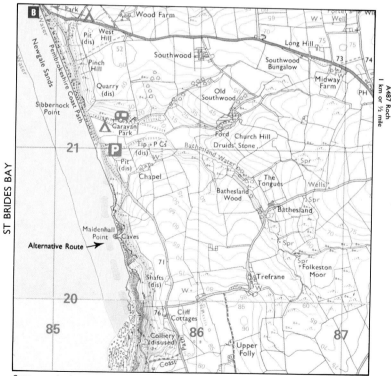

Contours are given in metres
The vertical interval is 5m

Trefrane Cliff Colliery was worked from 1850 to 1905, with coal exported from Nolton Haven by sea and also from Haverfordwest. The coal was hauled initially in pairs of 8-ton trolleys by traction engines. You can see good traces of the colliery remains – the brick chimney stack, the foundations of the engine shed, the overgrown shaft, and piles of colliery waste and steam engine clinker. To the south you encounter many other traces of old coal workings. Rickets Head, with its characteristic profile projecting out into St Bride's Bay, should be renamed 'Rickety Head' since it is crumbling away, attacked on both sides by wave action.

Nolton Haven **37** (originally called 'Old Town') was one of the main coal-exporting points for the Nolton–Newgale Coalfield. Nolton village is located half a mile (1 km) from the beach, which has good clean sands, safe bathing (but look out for currents at certain states of the tide), a good car park, and toilets. The inn and the village shop are located close to the beach.

At Madoc's Haven the proper path (at the top of the slope) has been fenced off and a new path created lower down **C**. This is the one you should follow. Druidston Haven **38** is named not after a druid but after Drue, one of the Norman knights who established himself in this area in the early 12th century.

You must now follow the track to the road, and then take the road uphill past Druidston Villa before returning to the cliff top **D**. There is a path in front of Druidston Villa and along the coast, but it is private. If you are still to be convinced about the effects of marine erosion, take a careful look at this stretch of coastline! When you reach the coast it is worth taking a slight detour to the north to look at the cliff scenery, before continuing southward on the Coast Path proper. Between Druidston Caves and Haroldston Chins you can see a range of quite spectacular cliff-collapse features – clifftop crevasses, rock falls, pinnacles, towers, stepped and faulted cliff faces, scree slopes and detached blocks. South of Haroldston Chins the vegetated cliff slope is littered with great blocks of rock.

On Black Point there is a simple Iron Age fort in a far from simple position. There are two hut circles on the peninsula. Look carefully at the landscape hereabouts, for it shows how rapidly certain processes can operate to change the appearance of the land surface. Modern landslides, which started in 1944 and continued in the 1960s, have transformed the landscape; in effect, the whole peninsula has dropped seawards. The landslide crevasses and escarpments can be seen adjacent to the

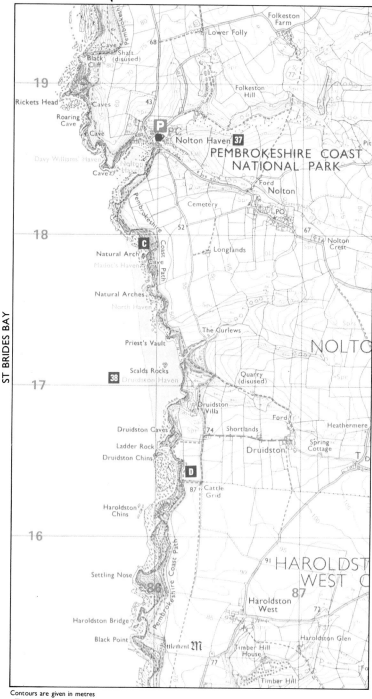

Contours are given in metres
The vertical interval is 5m

81

footpath. About half a mile further south, the Sleek Stone is a textbook example of a monocline, jutting out of the cliffs and easily seen from the footpath.

Broad Haven **39** has been a popular bathing beach since the early 1800s. The National Park Information Centre, formerly the Pembrokeshire Countryside Unit, was opened in 1970 as a pioneering enterprise in the popular interpretation of the natural environment. Next door is the large and well-appointed youth hostel, and along the sea front to the south you will find a hotel, shop, post office and inn.

Little Haven **40** is a pretty holiday village and one-time coal port, which owes most of its growth to the 19th-century exploitation of the coal-bearing rocks to the south and east. The modern settlement is confined within a deep, narrow valley. There are inns, shops and a large car park, but road access is difficult via very steep hills on all sides.

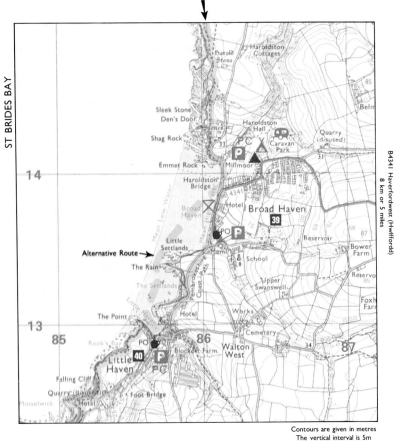

Contours are given in metres
The vertical interval is 5m

The Pembrokeshire coal industry

The Pembrokeshire Coalfield is part of the South Wales Coalfield, isolated from the main coal-mining area and with the coalbearing strata compressed and broken in such a way that exploitation has always been difficult. Nevertheless, Pembrokeshire was famous as the source of the world's finest anthracite, and it is said that Queen Victoria refused to allow coal from anywhere else to fire the boilers of her royal yachts.

Coal was being worked in crude open pits as far back as the 14th century, and traces of these old pits can still be found in the three main coal-mining districts – at the head of St Bride's Bay around Newgale, Nolton and Little Haven; around the inner part of the Milford Haven waterway; and in the Saundersfoot–Amroth area. By 1600, pits were being worked everywhere as the use of anthracite for domestic heating became more and more popular, and by 1700 demand was growing further afield. Soon coal was the main export from the Pembrokeshire ports, and for 200 years it was the basis for most of the industrial activity of the county. By 1800 the coalfield had attained national importance and demand ran far ahead of supply. During the early 1800s annual production totals in excess of 150,000 tons were achieved regularly, but after 1865 production fell off gradually in the face of competition from the larger British coalfields. Also, the Pembrokeshire mines were never very well equipped, and underground conditions were appalling because of the narrow and fractured coal seams and because of drainage problems as shafts were driven deeper and deeper. Nevertheless, some of the collieries continued working until the present century, and the last mine, at Hook, was in use until 1948.

There are at least 140 abandoned mines in Pembrokeshire, and literally hundreds of abandoned bell-pits. Piles of colliery spoil can be seen from the Coast Path around Newgale, Nolton, Saundersfoot and Amroth; other relics of the industry include the stack of Trefrane Cliff Colliery near Newgale and Saundersfoot Harbour, which once looked down on a beach pitch black with coal dust.

7 Little Haven to Dale (via St Ann's Head)

passing Musselwick and Marloes Sands
20¼ miles (32.7 km)

You can reach Little Haven **40** by a regular bus service from Haverfordwest and Broad Haven; the bus stop is at the top of the hill to the north of the village. Starting this section of the walk in the centre of the village, follow the track out towards The Point and turn left on to the Coast Path.

The gentle and well protected cliffs on the way to Borough Head come as a pleasant surprise, covered with glorious deciduous woodland. A path leaves the trail to descend the cliffs to the site of an abandoned sailing lifeboat station which operated between 1882 and 1922. As you approach Borough Head **41**, look at the tree crowns. Salt spray and wind blasting have killed many of the topmost branches.

ST BRIDES BAY

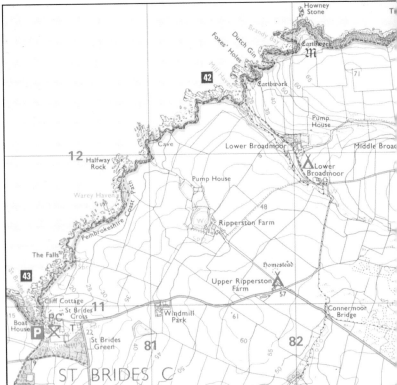

Contours are given in met
The vertical interval is 5

To the west of Borough Head **41** the coast is more exposed, and the path takes you eventually to the evocatively named inlets of Brandy Bay and Dutch Gin. Foxes' Hole is another inlet, this time cut along a great fault. Mill Haven **42** is a small, attractive cove accessible on foot from Lower Broadmoor Farm. The cove is chiefly notable now for its sculpture by Alain Ayres.

St Bride's Haven **43** is a pretty cove occupying the northern end of a broad valley that runs across the peninsula towards Dale. It offers bright red cliffs, a 'Victorianised' church, two walled gardens, and a large and well-built lime kiln. There is room to park up to 30 cars, and grassy banks for picnics. In the cliffs near the lime kiln, coastal retreat has exposed the ends of stone-lined coffins in the old graveyard. This is stately home territory. St Bride's Estate once belonged to the Barons of Kensington. Attractive parkland surrounds the Victorian 'castle' which was the baronial residence.

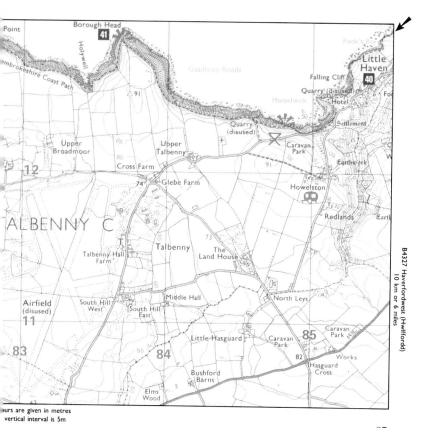

ours are given in metres
vertical interval is 5m

B4327 Haverfordwest (Hwlffordd)
10 km or 6 miles

The national trail follows the seaward boundary wall of the estate towards The Nab Head **44**, which is the site of Pembrokeshire's best-known Mesolithic flint-chipping floor. The name derives from the old word 'knap', meaning the process of striking flakes off flint nodules. To the south of Tower Point the Kensington Estate wall is particularly impressive. Note the buttresses and measures taken to continue the line of the wall across a deep gulley.

Musselwick Bay **45** has a lovely golden sandy beach, with reasonable access down a steep gulley. The beach is backed by high, dark-coloured, crumbly cliffs – do not get cut off by a rising tide, and do watch out for rock falls. There is good footpath access from the Marloes–Martin's Haven road.

Now the path takes you westwards along a fascinating stretch of coast with craggy rock outcrops on the cliff slopes. Soon you come to Martin's Haven **46**, the departure point for the Skomer Island boats and the 'port' for the village of Marloes. Very popular nowadays with the sub-aqua fraternity, it has a car park, toilets, and a sales point and information centre for the Dyfed Wildlife Trust. There is an inscribed Celtic ring-cross (more than 1,000 years old) in the Deer Park wall near the cottage.

The Deer Park **47** is contained by a stone wall built around 1800 as an embellishment to the St Bride's Estate. The wall runs parallel to an Iron Age embankment on the western side of a

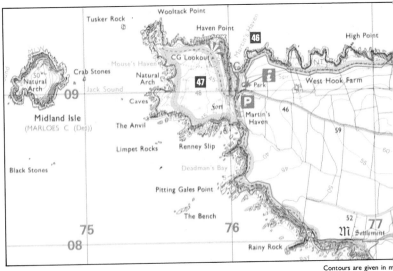

Contours are given in m
The vertical interval is

glacial meltwater channel. Explore the Deer Park if you have time. Out to the west you can see Midland Isle with Skomer beyond; and further away, to the south-west, Skokholm (see page 132). Note also how the heathland in the centre of the peninsula gives way to coastal grassland, with thrift and prostrate broom on the exposed cliff edges.

From Renney Slip, follow the trail towards Rainy Rock and Albion Sands, passing a promontory fort with triple embank-

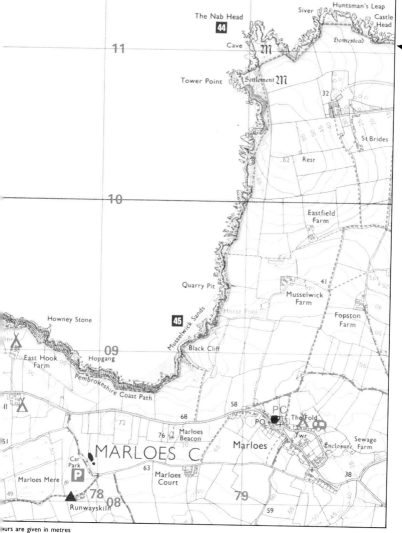

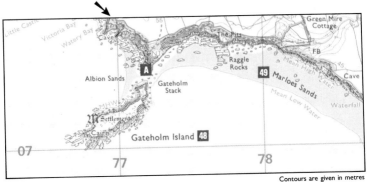

Contours are given in metres
The vertical interval is 5m

ments and a good settlement platform. When you reach the promontory adjacent to Gateholm **A** you will encounter a footpath leading inland to the Marloes Sands Youth Hostel and car park. Here you can escape from the Coast Path if you do not wish to walk all the way to Dale.

The mainland promontory (Horse Neck) and Gateholm Island are made of Old Red Sandstone – the colour of the rocks is unmistakable. Beware of the tide if you cross to the island **48**. Gateholm once supported a sizeable population, and there are 130 hut-circles, indicating settlement in the Iron Age. Later, in the Age of the Saints, there may have been a Christian monastic community here.

Marloes Sands **49** is one of the most beautiful Pembrokeshire beaches. There is good, safe bathing when the weather is calm. Access is via a sunken lane and down the stream valley from the National Trust car park. At Three Chimneys, beds of alternating sandstone and mudstone stand almost vertically, with the 'chimneys' picked out by differential erosion.

The national trail continues along the cliff tops, providing fine views of the beach below. As you approach Red Cliff you come upon the old RAF Dale aerodrome, later a Fleet Air Arm station, HMS *Goldcrest*, which closed in 1948. It is easy walking above Red Cliff and Hooper's Point. At The Hookses you may be surprised by the cottage nestling in its valley. There was also a farm here before the upper part of the valley was transformed by the building of the airfield.

Westdale Bay occupies the western end of an old river valley on the line of the Ritec fault, which extends eastwards along the Milford Haven waterway from Dale. Bathing is dangerous; beware of a strong undertow on an ebbing tide. From here **B** you can either follow the path inland to Dale or continue southwards on the trail. The full circuit of the peninsula will add about 5 miles (8 km) and 3 hours to your walk. On the south shore of Westdale Bay, Great Castle Head supports a late Iron Age promontory fort. Around Long Point and Short Point you encounter many traces of ruined buildings. This was the site of HMS *Harrier*, a Royal Navy radar and meteorological school. South of Short Point, a gap in the National Trust embankment leads to the free Trust car park at Kete. This is a good start/finish point for those walking the full circuit of the Dale Peninsula.

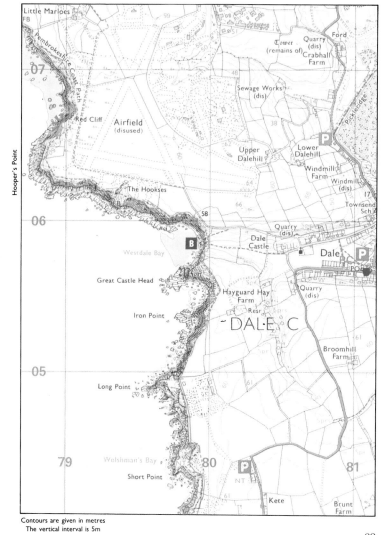

Contours are given in metres
The vertical interval is 5m

The western end of Marloes Sands, with the ancient settlement site of Gateholm

the distance.

Above a little creek called The Vomit **50** the path joins the road from Dale. Here, on the southernmost tip of the Dale peninsula, there is no public access to the cliff tops because of the coastguard and Trinity House installations. St Ann's Head guards the approach to the Milford Haven waterway. On the western flank of the little peninsula is the coastguard station, installed in 1966 in one of the two old lighthouses which closed in 1910. Now the converted building is the Milford Haven Maritime Rescue Sub-Centre, the co-ordinating centre for all coastal and maritime emergencies around the Pembrokeshire coast. The front light, lower down and closer to the tip of the headland, was built in 1841 as a replacement for an old coal-fired light tower. You may walk south towards the lighthouse, but must then use the small gate in front of the round engine house and follow the marked path northwards across the field **C**. Do not follow the cliff tops. You will see an attractive row of coastguard and Trinity House cottages (they are now in private ownership). The walled garden and steps and the quay were built in 1800 for the import of building materials for the lighthouses and cottages.

Mill Bay **51** is where Henry Tudor landed with 2,000 men on 7th August 1485. From here he marched through Wales, and 15 days after his landing he and his allies won the famous battle for the English crown at Bosworth Field. From Mill Bay you follow the path eastwards. Close to three navigation towers (used by ships entering Milford Haven) there are gun emplacements associated with West Blockhouse. This open battery was in use during both World Wars. West Blockhouse itself has been sensitively restored by the Landmark Trust for holiday letting.

Watwick Bay is a surprise, with clean golden sands, good bathing and a lush wooded valley. To the north-east, the Watwick Point light, about 160 feet (50 metres) high, is one of the essential navigational features maintained by the Port Authority for waterway shipping. Castlebeach Bay is at the mouth of another lush wooded valley, where you will find a ruined lime kiln. There is a small sandy beach, suitable for bathing.

Dale Fort **52** is Victorian, having been built as a component of the Haven defences between 1852 and 1856. Since 1947 the fort has belonged to the Field Studies Council. When you reach the road leading to the fort, turn left. As you walk you can look down into a dense deciduous woodland, well sheltered from the prevailing south-westerlies and far enough from the west coast to escape the worst effects of salt spray.

Dale **53** is an old trading and fishing port, one of the largest settlements of the Haven in Tudor times. Fishing, shipbuilding and general trading were the main activities, and the little port served a sizeable farming population. Now there are only three fishing boats in the village, and Dale has become a popular watersports centre. The beach is stony and rough, and there is inadequate parking for cars and boats, but these problems do not deter hordes of summer visitors. There are toilets, shops, a chandlery, café, public house, and Dale Yacht Club.

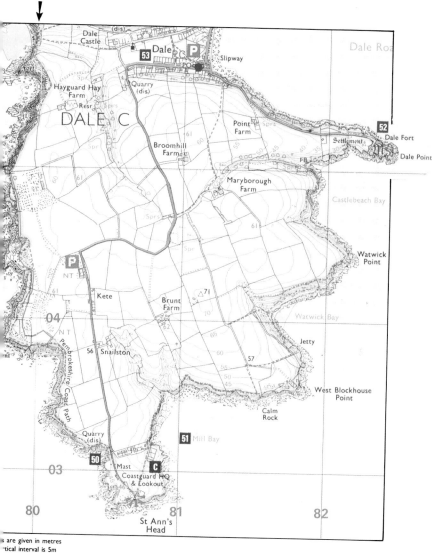

are given in metres
·tical interval is 5m

A CIRCULAR WALK TO MARLOES SANDS AND MARTIN'S HAVEN

6½ miles (10.5 km)

Start and finish at the Runwayskiln car park about half a mile (1 km) west of Marloes village. The walk allows a couple of options for reducing its length, but reckon on a full day if you want to take your time and absorb the beauties of this splendid peninsula. The walk is described anticlockwise. Walk north to the main road and turn right towards Marloes Beacon. Look out for the left turn off the road, which will take you down to Musslewick Sands. Then follow the national trail westwards all the way to Martin's Haven. There is an alternative start/finish point here, in the Martin's Haven car park. You should make a point of exploring the Deer Park **47**. This was the largest Iron Age defended settlement site in Pembrokeshire. As far as we

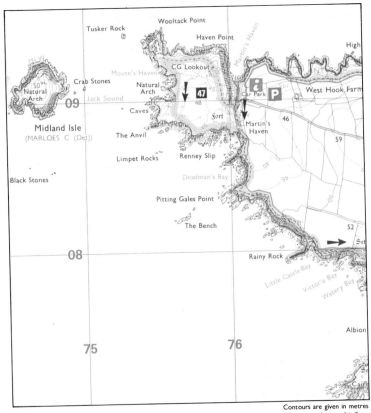

Contours are given in metres
The vertical interval is 5m

know, the Deer Park was never populated with deer. If you follow the path around the park you are rewarded with wonderful views of the coast, with Midland Isle and Skomer Island beyond.

Continue from Renney Slip towards Albion Sands, where you can descend to the beach. When the tide is low, you can clamber up on to Gateholm **48** if you are feeling energetic. Now you have three options: you can take the footpath past Marloes Mere to the youth hostel and thence back to the car park; follow Marloes Sands beach **49** east towards the mouth of the stream (at low tide only); or follow the national trail along the cliff top. Once you reach the mouth of the stream, the footpath is well-worn, running uphill to the sunken lane and then more gently uphill back to your starting point.

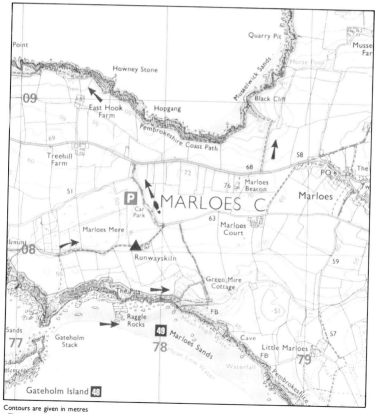

Contours are given in metres
The vertical interval is 5m

8 Dale to Neyland

via Monk Haven and Milford Haven
16 miles (25.7 km)

Dale **53** is not easy to reach by public transport, although there are weekly bus services linking the village with Haverfordwest and Milford Haven. The walk to Neyland takes you through oil refining country and also through an urban stretch in and around Milford Haven. There are a number of points at which care is needed if you are not to lose contact with the Coast Path.

Start this stretch of the national trail in Dale village, following the road northwards along the shore of the Gann Estuary. After about half a mile you will come to the Pickleridge car park **A**, passing two ruined lime kilns on your left. There are not many windmill remains left in Pembrokeshire, but behind you on the hillside is one of them. Probably it was used for corn milling.

Before setting off from the Pickleridge car park to cover the stretch to Milford Haven, think very carefully about your timings. Consultation of the tide tables is essential. There are two places at which you have to cross tidal creeks – The Gann and Sandy Haven, both of which are submerged for most of the time. At The Gann you have four hours around low water in which to cross, and the same timings apply at Sandy Haven. It will take you about two hours to walk between the two. So you should leave Pickleridge on a falling tide. If you get your timings wrong, you will have to walk three times as far to reach the eastern side of Sandy Haven, or else wade (or swim!) across Sandy Haven Creek.

The 'high-water detour' at The Gann is as follows. Take the road northwards to Mullock Bridge; cross the bridge and take the Milford Haven fork **B**; opposite Mullock Farm entrance turn right and follow the path as far as Slatehill Farm. Turn right at the farm and descend to the estuary. Then follow the estuary southwards to rejoin the Coast Path near The Gann.

On the west side of Pickleridge the lagoons are flooded gravel pits created in 1941–42 during the phase of wartime airfield construction. On the seaward side of the ridge are the extensive intertidal Gann Flats, widely used by marine biology students based at Dale Fort.

Having reached the eastern side of the estuary you can either walk along the shoreline or take the path along the field boundary, east and then swinging south, and then down the track. If you follow the shore, look out for the fingerposts showing where the Coast Path leaves the beach.

Monk Haven **54** is a surprise and a joy. The lovely wooded valley runs up towards the village of St Ishmael's. The massive castellated wall that runs across the valley at high-tide level was built as part of the Trewarren Estate, probably in the 1700s. On the east side of the creek the watch tower near the point is a Victorian folly. Around Watch House Point there is an assortment of lookout and artillery positions dating from the First World War, both above and below the trail. These provide shelter in case of bad weather.

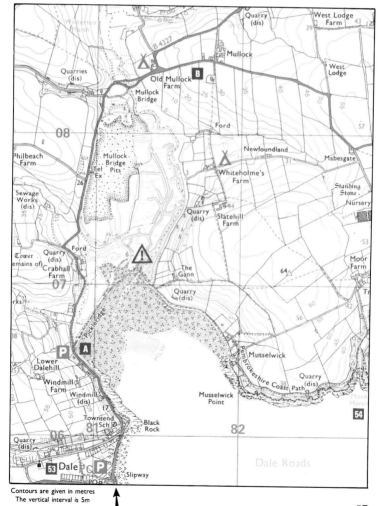

Contours are given in metres
The vertical interval is 5m

Contours are given in
The vertical interval

Lindsway Bay, accessible via a steep path and easily reached by the footpath from St Ishmael's, is chiefly notable as the place where HRH The Prince of Wales first set foot on Welsh soil in 1955.

As you follow the trail south-eastwards, you come to Great Castle Head, which has an extensive Iron Age fort defended by

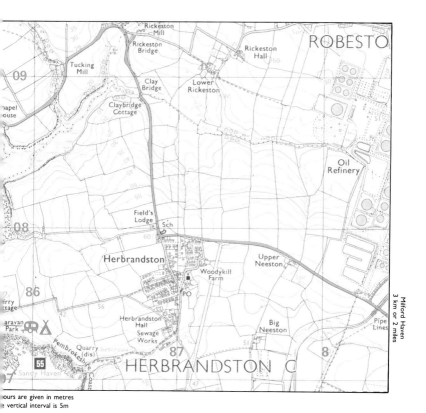

Milford Haven
3 km or 2 miles

ours are given in metres
e vertical interval is 5m

a single embankment and ditch. The buildings and scanning radar out on the headland are part of the waterway navigational system.

Sandy Haven **55** can be reached by road via Sandy Haven Farm, or via the village of Herbrandston. There are a few cottages here, on the western side of the creek near the old ferry landing. This is a lovely spot, with Sandyhaven Pill emptied and filled with every tidal cycle. If your timing is right (you have four hours), you can now cross the 'bridge' without getting your feet wet; if not, you have a very long detour inland around the Pill.

The high-water detour is as follows. Take the road northwards past Sandy Haven Farm. Turn right on reaching the Dale–Milford road, and follow this road via Rickeston Bridge and Clay Bridge to Herbrandston. At the village hall follow the footpath sign, turning right to follow the lane down to the Pill. Then follow the shore southwards, skirting the caravan park and walking along the clifftop footpath.

South of Sandy Haven beach you cannot escape the influence of the Milford Haven oil industry. The great embankments near the national trail belong to the Esso refinery **56**, which ceased production in 1983. Most of the tanks, and the refining complex itself, have now been cleared. Adjacent to the path you will see a series of old gun emplacements from the First World War. Offshore you can see Stack Rock Fort, one of the Victorian defences of the waterway. In its heyday (1870) it supported an armament of 23 turret guns and a garrison of 168 men. South Hook Fort, located on the landward side of the Coast Path, was completed in 1863, and was designed so that its batteries could complement those of Stack Rock Fort. The defensible barracks, whose massive bulk can be glimpsed over the 'cosmetic' embankment built by Esso, had a garrison of 180 men.

As you pass under the landward end of the Esso jetty, you leave the national park. Follow the road past the housing estate and downhill past the Amoco jetty access point.

Gelliswick Bay is the headquarters of the Pembrokeshire Yacht Club, and the local beach for the communities of Hubberston and Hakin. It is dominated to the west by the Amoco

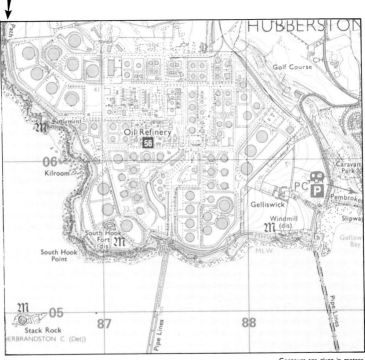

Contours are given in metres
The vertical interval is 5m

jetty and to the east by Fort Hubberston. This particular fort, completed in 1865, had a garrison of 250 men, and the gun emplacements (as at South Hook Fort) supported 28 guns.

Halfway up the hill **C**, turn right up the steps, follow the track adjacent to the school playing field, turn right at the school, and then follow the most obvious route to the Victoria Bridge at the head of Milford Docks. This means following Picton Road, Spike's Lane and St Anne's Road. Look out for the acorn symbols on the pavements.

Milford Docks **57** have had a chequered history. The new town of Milford was planned in 1790, with the docks as the focus. Originally it was planned to establish a naval dockyard here and to develop the Irish packet trade, but money was in short supply and both the Admiralty and the Irish Mail moved to Pembroke Dock. The docks were not completed until 1888. Hopes of attracting transatlantic passenger traffic never materialised, but gradually the town's fishing industry expanded and between 1900 and 1914 Milford joined the top league of fishing ports. Now there are only a few trawlers based here, and the docks are kept alive by general trading and ship-repairing.

Follow Hamilton Terrace along the lower edge of the town. The street is named after Sir William Hamilton, the town's founder, who died in 1803. Turn right along the Rath and pass the Rock Gardens and old swimming pool. Follow Murray Road and then turn right down Beach Hill. Take the path below the housing estate and you will eventually gain access to the

Contours are given in metres
The vertical interval is 5m

western shore of Castle Pill. On the western side of the Pill entrance you can see the old Ward's shipbreaking yard, while to the east are the substantial buildings of the Royal Naval Armaments Depot, established in 1934. At the Dudley Marine boatyard, follow the shore northwards if the tide is right, or take the road to the causeway which crosses the Pill.

Having crossed Black Bridge, follow the B4325 up the hill and towards Waterston. This is a dangerous stretch – there is no pavement and traffic travels fast. Near Hill Crest cottage, turn right **D** and follow the lane southwards to Venn Farm, then follow the fingerposts. The national trail is easy to follow along the southern edge of the Gulf refinery (2 miles/3.2 km). The extraordinary iron cage, which takes you across the pipeline run connecting jetty and refinery, is yet another of the footpath's eccentric surprises. You continue to another extraordinary footbridge over the jetty approach road, and the Coast Path drops down to sea level to the east of Wear Point. You then continue with a pleasant, easy walk towards Hazelbeach. There are several well-maintained seats and fine views across the waterway towards the Pembroke Power Station and Pembroke Dock, and upstream towards Cleddau Bridge.

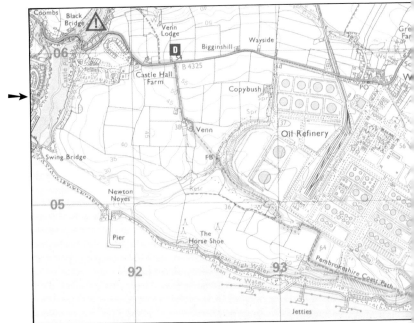

Contours are given in
The vertical interva

102

At Hazelbeach, close to the Ferry Inn, you will find toilets, car parking spaces, and access to the shore. Now you continue eastwards on the road, passing Llanstadwell Church with its typical castellated 'Little England' tower. Church and churchyard are beautifully situated right on the edge of the waterway. Turn right on to the main road (B4325), then go past the Neyland Yacht Club and the Brunel Hotel, and down to Brunel Quay.

Neyland **58**, like Milford, is a planned town, but about 50 years younger. It owes its origin to Isambard Kingdom Brunel, who made it the terminus for his South Wales Railway in 1856. For almost half a century the town thrived, with a fishing industry, ice factory, shipyard, and busy sea traffic for the Irish packet service. Lord Beeching's famous axe fell upon the railway in 1955, and 20 years later the ferry service disappeared as well. Now, after a period of decline, Neyland is picking up again. Brunel Quay, once busy with rail sidings and quayside activity, has seen a carefully planned resurgence. The marina was the catalyst, and now there is a large car park, a terminus for pleasure cruises on the waterway, a chandlery, cafeteria and shop, new factory units and new housing developments.

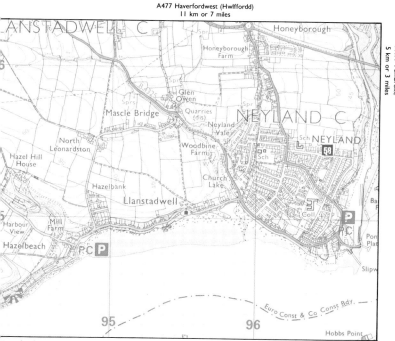

A477 Haverfordwest (Hwlffordd)
11 km or 7 miles

A477 Pembroke
5 km or 3 miles

s are given in metres
rtical interval is 5m

103

A CIRCULAR WALK TO GREAT CASTLE HEAD

3¾ miles (6 km)

Start and finish either at Sandy Haven **55** (very limited parking) or at the St Ishmael's Sports and Social Club at the western extremity of the walk. I will assume that you start from St Ishmael's, walking anticlockwise. This is an easy walk for an afternoon, with relatively little climbing. Follow the footpath along the western edge of the playing field, turn right and you will soon reach the national trail above Lindsway Bay. Follow the footpath south-eastwards towards Great Castle Head. (If you prefer a brief walk, turn left shortly after Rook's Nest Point and return to St Ishmael's.) Out on the headland, explore or simply follow the Iron Age bank across to the eastern side and then continue via Little Castle Head towards Sandy Haven **55**. The path (recently realigned here) runs through the woods on the western shore of the inlet. Descend to the beach if you wish, adjacent to the Sandy Haven cottages; then retrace your steps and follow the road past Skerryback Farm. Before you reach Bicton, take the left turn for St Ishmael's and return to the Sports Club.

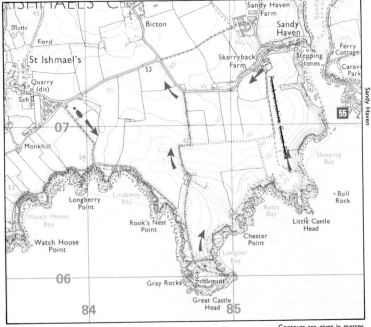

Contours are given in metres
The vertical interval is 5m

The Milford Haven oil industry

The oil industry came to Milford Haven in the late 1950s as the oil companies began to plan for the use of supertankers to transport Middle Eastern crude oil to Britain. These tankers were being designed to carry ever-larger tonnages, and deep-water berthing facilities were required that could handle vessels of 300,000 tons or more. Milford Haven appeared ideal for development. In 1957–58, work began on the creation of a major oil port right on the edge of the national park.

The first refinery to be built was the Esso refinery at Herbrandston, which came on-stream in 1960. The BP Ocean Terminal, on the south shore near the old Popton Point fort, was opened in 1961. Some land at Kilpaison in Angle Bay was used for a crude-oil tank-farm, but BP did not build a refinery here; instead they constructed a 62-mile (100-km) pipeline to their

Milford Docks, once one of the great centres of the British deep-sea fishing industry.

Castle Pill, Milford Haven, with the stacks of the Texaco refinery on the skyline.

Llandarcy refinery near Swansea, capable of pumping 10 million tons of crude oil per year. Next came the Texaco refinery near Pembroke, on the south shore of the Haven and a little further inland. This is the company's only UK refinery, and since its opening in October 1964 it has been expanded to handle 15 million tons of crude oil per year. In 1968 the Gulf Oil refinery was opened near Waterston, with a three-berth jetty quite close to the shore. This was the only Milford Haven refinery with an associated petrochemical plant. Finally, in 1973, the Amoco refinery came on-stream, the only one located away from the coast. It is served by a long jetty quite close to the Esso jetty and adjacent to Gelliswick Bay; all of the pipelines between the jetty and refinery are buried.

The oil industry has brought with it a variety of ancillary developments. The most prominent is the Pembroke power station, completed in 1975 and intended to burn heavy fuel oil for the generation of 2,000 megawatts for the grid, sufficient to meet the electricity requirements of the whole of South Wales. The huge chimney stack, 750 feet (230 metres) high, is visible from all over West Wales; and the double row of 400-kilovolt supergrid power lines makes a dramatic and not very beautiful impact on the Pembrokeshire landscape. Inland, the reservoir at Llysyfran was built to provide water for the oil industry. A pipeline was constructed to carry refined products to conveniently placed distribution centres in England, and the Milford Haven Conservancy Board (now the Port Authority) undertook a huge programme of rock dredging in the deep-water channel, together with the installation of transit lights and other navigational aids, some of which the walker passes on the Coast Path.

Recent changes in the oil industry include the closure of the Esso refinery in 1983, the closure of the BP Ocean Terminal shortly afterwards, and the cessation of petrochemical manufacture at the Gulf refinery. The rest of the industry appears relatively stable at present.

9 Neyland to Angle

through Pembroke Dock and Pembroke
17½ miles (28.2 km)

Neyland **58** is a convenient stopping/starting point, with good bus links from Haverfordwest, Milford Haven and Pembroke. The town centre is within easy walking distance of Brunel Quay **59**, where refreshments are available. To continue on the Coast Path follow the route of the old railway track past the marina and walk beneath the Westfield Pill bridge. Then climb up the track on your left until you reach the roadway. Turn left, cross the bridge and continue to the Cleddau Bridge proper. There is car parking space at the junction with the road to Burton Ferry.

The Cleddau Bridge was built between 1967 and 1975 in order to improve communications between the two shores of the waterway. As you cross the bridge, note the contrast between the views upstream and downstream.

You now embark upon a 'town trail' through Pembroke Dock. Follow the new road to the roundabout, turn right along the London Road, then left towards the town centre. Carry straight on if you want to explore the town. Otherwise turn right into the car park, pass the public library and get on to Front Street **A**. From this point on, look out for the acorn markers on the pavement. At the western end of Front Street is the massive defensive wall of the Royal Naval Dockyard **60** and the Martello tower, built around 1850, which was a part of the dockyard defensive system.

Turn left at the King's Arms and walk straight up Commercial Row, following the Pembroke signs. Turn left along Victoria Road and right along Bellevue Terrace. Carry straight on past Bethany Baptist Church, and continue downhill past the filling station. At the dip in the road **B**, there is no fingerpost, but follow the tarmac path off to your left, along the edge of a little valley. Continue down past the row of cottages, cross the stile, and follow the footpath proper, with your route pointed out again by a fingerpost. Be sure to turn left off the track where indicated; follow the fingerposts and do not continue towards the sea. For half a mile or so the path runs across farmland before entering woodland near Bush School. The limestone quarries in the woods were used to provide the stone for Pembroke Castle and the walls and other buildings of the medieval town.

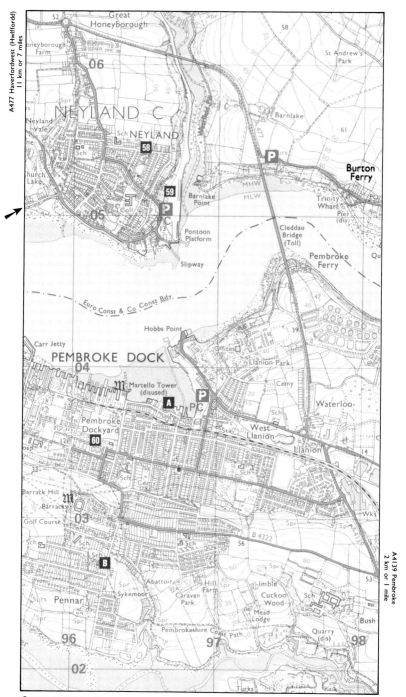

Contours are given in metres
The vertical interval is 5m

The national trail now takes you into the suburbs on the north side of the Pembroke town pond; when you reach the main road turn right and continue across the barrage into the town. Pembroke Castle **61** dominates the scene, and is one of the most powerful of the Norman fortresses in Wales. The present castle was built for the most part in the period 1190–1245 by William Marshal and his sons. Its most impressive feature is the Great Keep (the finest of its kind in Britain), which provides a commanding view in all directions. During the Middle Ages the castle was the key to the control of Little England, strategically located right in the heartland of the Anglo-Norman colony. It never fell to the Welsh. In 1457 Henry Tudor was born in the castle. The old walled town of Pembroke **62** was created by the Normans; traces of the walls can still be seen, especially around St Michael's Tower and on the south side of the town.

Follow the road past the castle and continue to Monkton. There are some fascinating buildings here – the Old Hall, the remains of the Old Priory, and the fine spacious church. If you wish you can turn right and take the pedestrianised lane past the Old Hall. The national trail then follows the B4320 road westwards.

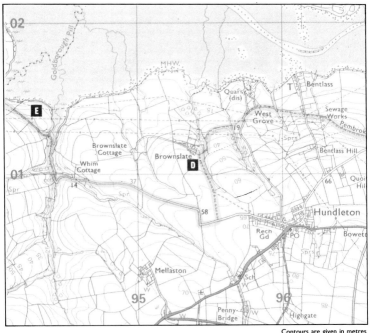

Contours are given in metres
The vertical interval is 5m

After half a mile or so leave the main road (do not continue round the corner) and drop down into the valley between the new bungalows **C**. Pass Quoits Mill Dam and follow the lane uphill. Turn right when you encounter the fingerpost.

Now, having bid farewell to the medieval splendours of Pembroke and Monkton, you return to the modern world! This is an electrical landscape; everything is dwarfed by the 180-foot (55-metre) pylons that carry the output of the Pembroke power station **63** eastwards to join the supergrid. Ahead you can see the power station's 750-foot (230-metre) chimney stack.

When you reach Brownslate you must follow the farm lane southwards **D**, although your instinct tells you that you should continue to head west. Turn right when you reach the road, and follow the road westwards for about half a mile (1 km). On rounding the corner after Whim Cottage, strike off the road and cross the stile on your right. Follow the little valley towards the head of Goldborough Pill; the path is very muddy and difficult to discern. Soon you will see a huge square lime kiln with hinges which held iron doors across the entrance. Now, after swinging west again, you come to the worst section of the Pembrokeshire Coast Path **E**. The lane is heavily used by cattle, as is the track down in the wooded valley of Lambeeth. Be prepared for *mud*.

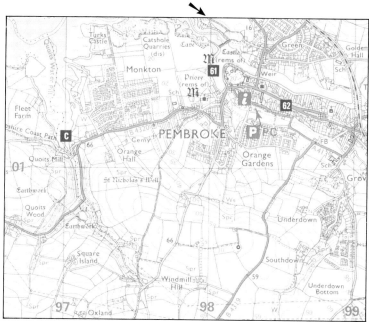

Contours are given in metres
The vertical interval is 5m

The view from the battlements of Pembroke Castle, with Pembroke power station

...nd the Texaco refinery in the distance.

The path climbs through Lambeeth Farm, and soon you can enjoy good views in all directions. To the east, Pembroke River estuary is a fine area for waders and other waterfowl, especially during the winter.

As you join the approach road to the power station **63** you will skirt the edge of a 'spare' power station site, kept in reserve by the Central Electricity Generating Board. Turn right off the road **F** and follow the path along the edge of the sports field. At stile 112, turn left and then right, following the road past Pwllcrochan Church. Beware – the footpath shown above the word 'Pwllcrochan' on the map does not exist, so follow the instructions in this guide rather than the map.

Martin's Haven inlet provides access on to Pwllcrochan Flats, once famous for their oyster and cockle fishery. If you feel like a short detour you can walk down to the shore on the western side of the creek, leaving the road adjacent to the bridge. Near the bridge, wild celery and marshmallow grow on the salt marsh.

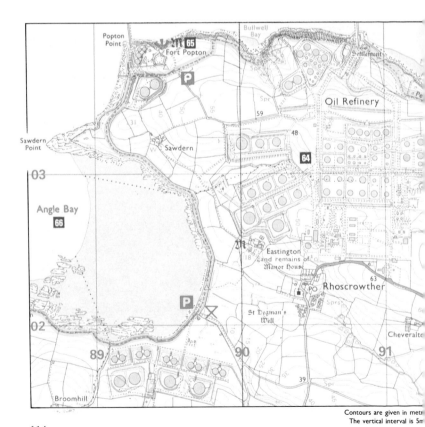

Contours are given in metr
The vertical interval is 5m

Continue along the lane, heading north-west. From the field at the end you have an excellent view of the Texaco refinery **64**, which is now, following the Esso closure, the largest refinery on the Haven.

After traversing several fields, the path descends and then runs under the base of the jetty. It has five berths, the largest of which can handle 300,000-ton supertankers.

The path continues via Bullwell Bay. As you climb out of the bay you pass the redundant jetty once used for the import of crude oil to the BP Ocean Terminal. Soon you approach Fort Popton **65**, another of the Victorian defences of the waterway, built around 1860. After the closure of the BP Ocean Terminal the building was empty for some years, but it now houses a Field Studies Council Research Centre.

Continue past the old oil tank site and descend towards the shore of Angle Bay **66**. Walking is easy on the asphalt service road built by BP. There is a picnic site and car parking near the old pumping station. At this point you have to descend to the foreshore and follow it for the next 1½ miles (2.5 km). The foreshore is stony and often slippery, so the going is difficult.

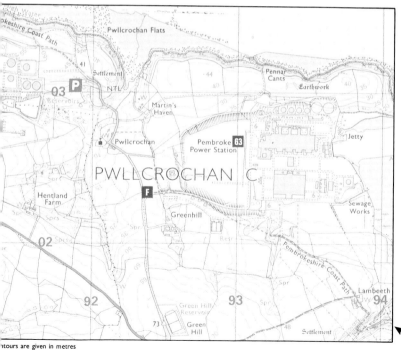

ntours are given in metres
he vertical interval is 5m

Angle Bay **66** and its extensive mudflats are important winter feeding grounds for birds. There are many different habitats: calcareous mudflats, saltings, bare intertidal rocky areas, gravel beds and coarse pebble beaches. Eventually, with some relief, you can climb up off the beach and walk above the wall towards Angle.

The little creek **67** is charming, with a ruined quay, old harbour walls, and a long gravel ridge projecting out from the northern shore. There are always a few small boats here, and there are traces of two rotting hulks. The footbridge **G** marked on the map no longer exists; you are *not* advised to try to take a shortcut to the public house on the way to Angle Point! Continue to the village on the southern side of the creek.

Angle **68** is a single-street village flanked by remnants of the medieval strip-field system. The map shows how the main hedge boundaries run up-slope, at right angles to the main road. There are a number of interesting buildings, including the Georgian-style Globe Hotel, a fortified tower house, a medieval dovecote, and the remains of a supposed nunnery on the south side of the road. At the back of the church is a little Fisherman's Chapel above a vaulted crypt, built in 1447. The village has inns and a post office/shop, but accommodation is limited.

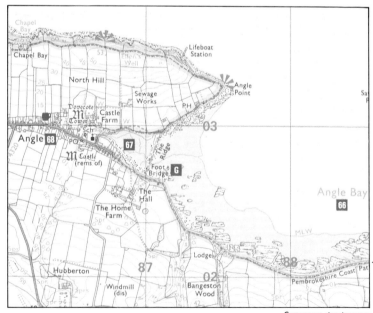

Contours are given in metres
The vertical interval is 5m

The Royal Naval Dockyard

The Royal Naval Dockyard at Pembroke Dock, begun in 1814, was at one time the finest and most innovative shipbuilding yard in the world. It was located here partly because of the sheltered deep-water anchorage, partly because of its remoteness from France, and partly because of a long tradition of local shipbuilding on the waterway.

It grew rapidly, and because it was a strategically safe base for technological experiments, vessels were soon being built with steam propulsion, with paddles and with screw propellers, and with iron cladding. Warships were also increasing rapidly in size. The year 1834 saw the launching of the *Tartarus*, the Navy's first steam man-of-war. The *Conflict* of 1846 was the first warship fitted with a screw propeller. In 1847 the yard launched the *Lion*, the Navy's largest warship. In 1852 the *Duke of Wellington* was launched, being the largest three-decker in the world.

Five royal yachts were built here, and year after year naval barques, brigantines, cruisers, gunboats and battleships were completed for the fleet. In all, the dockyard saw the construction of more than 250 naval vessels, with a peak output of 23 ships in a single year. In the later years of the 19th century, at the peak of its fame, the dockyard employed over 3,000 men. Around the turn of the century the dockyard specialised in cruisers and battleships, and submarines were also built here during the First World War. But after the war, shipbuilding activity declined sharply so the Navy abruptly closed the yard in 1925, heralding an era of severe local hardship.

During the Second World War the dockyard saw a new lease of life, with some ship-repairing work and the co-ordination of mine-laying, mine-sweeping and Atlantic convoy escort work. Pembroke Dock had a major Sunderland flying-boat base, and important fuel storage depots were established at Llanion and Llanreath. However, the military installations inevitably attracted enemy attention, and the town suffered heavily from air raids, particularly in 1940–41.

Since the war the dockyard has had a chequered history, but much of it is still in use and the western part remains in the possession of the Admiralty. The great defensive walls of the dockyard are more or less intact; the Martello towers still stand sentinel where the dockyard walls reach the sea; and many of the dock basins and solid Victorian dockyard buildings can be seen very close to the recommended route through the town.

10 Angle to Bosherston

negotiating the Castlemartin firing ranges
18 miles (29 km)

There is a weekday bus service to Angle, linking the village with Pembroke and Pembroke Dock. There is limited car parking in the village **68**. The first part of this walk follows the coast, with interesting and varied cliff scenery. The second part involves a long inland detour on the periphery of the Ministry of Defence firing range. Try to arrange this walk for a weekend; this will at least allow you to visit part of the limestone coast of the Castlemartin peninsula.

You start this stretch on the North Hill circuit by walking eastwards towards Angle Point. The Old Point House Inn (supposedly 16th century) is one of the few inns on the national trail, and very atmospheric. The pub fire is reputed never to have gone out during the last 300 years. Just off the path is the old lifeboat station, clearly recognisable in spite of its ruinous condition. The modern lifeboat station, opposite the redundant Esso jetty, is the only one on the Haven, well sheltered from the south-westerlies.

Continuing westwards, you pass in front of the Chapel Bay cottages and then, following the track, on the landward side of Chapel Bay Fort. The tall mast nearby is a Port Authority communications mast. Soon Thorn Island comes into view. The island fort (built in the 1850s) is still in a good state of repair. It is now a hotel for those who *really* want to get away from it all.

West Angle Bay **69** is a classic geological site. Look at the complicated geological structures and changes of rock type in the little coves on the north side of the bay. At the head of the beach there is a car park, telephone, toilets, caravan park and café. Behind the café are the remains of the brickworks; clay was excavated from a pit beside the toilet block.

Continuing westwards, you come across a disused RAF radio station, with old buildings and radio masts much in evidence. The modern building, formerly an RAF radar station, is now used for university radar research into offshore wave characteristics. Nearby, in a sweep overlooking the coast, are the gun emplacements of East Block House **70**, built around 1854. The old building that teeters on the edge of the cliff is the Elizabethan East Block House, built soon after the Spanish Armada sent a shiver down the spine of Britain.

Do not try to follow the coast to the south of East Block House **A**. Keep to the track marked with stakes, which runs past the Victorian battery and reaches the coast again near stile 84. On the mainland adjacent to Sheep Island you come across an Iron Age defended site, and a lookout post dating from 1914–18. Across a rather dangerous isthmus there is an extensive area with hut-circles and platforms, but it is not for the faint-hearted. There are further settlement traces on Sheep Island. As on Gateholm, the huts seem to have been built during the Age of the Saints. As you walk south-eastwards you see traces inland of Angle airfield **71**, built in the winter of 1940–41.

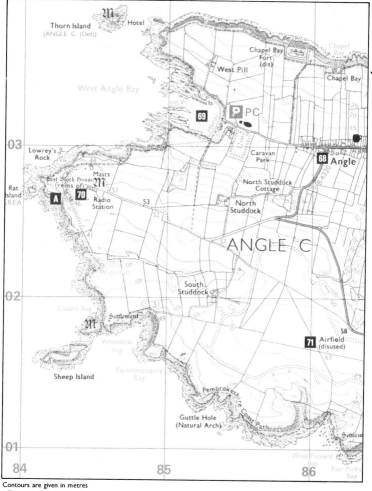

Contours are given in metres
The vertical interval is 5m

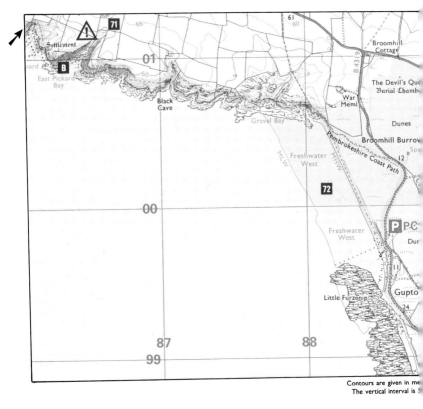

Contours are given in me
The vertical interval is !

Pick your way along the west side of East Pickard Bay wherever you feel inclined **B**, among the great jumble of Old Red Sandstone outcrops and fallen blocks. From either side of the bay there are views of the huge embankment being built along the southern edge of Angle airfield **71**. The path is steep and slippery in places; be very careful in wet weather.

Now, after a further half-mile or so, you reach Freshwater West **72**, one of the most spectacular bays in Pembrokeshire, with a superb sweep of sands extending for about $2\frac{1}{2}$ miles (4 km). The beach may look inviting, but beware of a very dangerous undertow on the ebb tide, and also of quicksands near the north end of the beach around low-water mark. Freshwater West is famous for its sand dunes, known as burrows.

This was once a great area for the collection of 'laver bread' from the intertidal rock outcrops. The thatched seaweed-drying hut on the grassy bank above Little Furzenip is the last one in Pembrokeshire, rescued and preserved by the National Park Authority a few years ago.

From Little Furzenip the intertidal area around Great Furzenip and on Frainslake Sands is within the Ministry of Defence firing ranges and out of bounds. You must follow the road (B4319) into Castlemartin. Castlemartin village has an inn, a substantial castle mound and a magnificent cattle pound. There was a pound here in 1480, but the present one dates from 1780 and was restored in 1972.

CASTLEMARTIN RANGE WARNING

All visitors to Castlemartin Range must note that this a Ministry of Defence Range and the public have no right of access when firing is taking place.

General instructions
1. Keep within waymarks on each path. Do not leave these marked paths.
2. Comply with the public notices at all times.
3. Do not touch or pick up any ammunition or any other object you may see.
4. Please do not enter any buildings.
5. Please protect the wildlife. Do not take specimens.
6. Camping or making fires is not permitted.

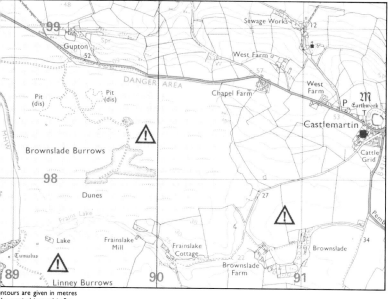

ntours are given in metres
he vertical interval is 5m

Broomhill Burrows, an area of dunes at Freshwater West formed from sand

...ains blown inland from the beach.

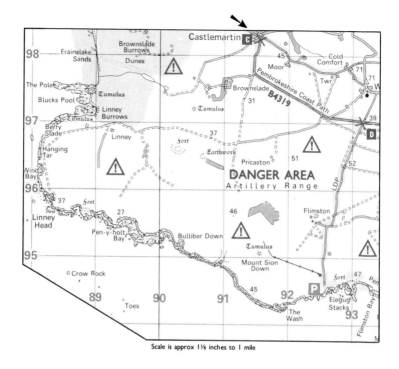

Scale is approx 1⅛ inches to 1 mile

It is always advisable to check the range firing schedules before proceeding beyond Castlemartin; see the local press for details of firing times or ask for information at any tourist information centre.

From Castlemartin, if the B4319 south is closed at gate **C** due to range activity, you will have to proceed east to Warren past the restored church with its tall steeple, and thence to Merrion Camp **73** to join the B4319 again. Warren Church was derelict for many years, but a daunting restoration project has now been completed and the church was opened again for worship in 1988. Merrion Camp **73** was established to provide training facilities and firing ranges for troops of the Royal Armoured Corps.

At the Merrion junction with the B4319 there are two possible routes. If the road to Stack Rocks is closed at gate **D** due to range activity, you will have to turn left and continue along the public road to Bosherston via Sampson Cross. However, if the road to Stack Rocks is open, then turn right at the camp entrance and walk along the B4319 to the first crossroads, where you turn left through gate **D**.

If the B4319 from Castlemartin is open and you arrive at gate **D** via this route, turn right towards Stack Rocks. Head south

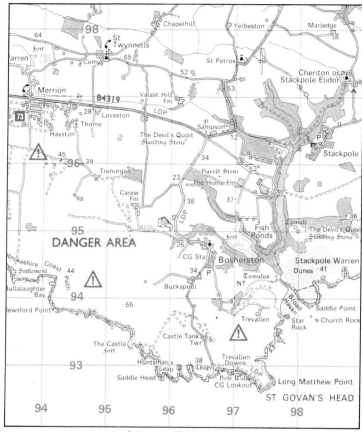

Scale is approx 1⅛ inches to 1 mile

from the crossroads through gate **D** for 1½ miles (2.5 km) to the Stack Rocks car park. Flimston Chapel is worth visiting en route to the coast, and is open in the summer months. Flimston Farm, adjacent to the church, will soon be opened to the public by the National Park Authority.

The path from grid ref. 915978 through Brownslade Farm and on around the coast to grid ref. 926946 (see page 133) is out of bounds to the public. However, during the year there are some 25 special guided walks organised by the National Park Authority. Contact any tourist information centre for more information.

There is pleasant clifftop walking as you turn eastwards to follow the south shore of the Castlemartin peninsula. If you are careful you can walk close to the cliff edge.

Probably the most photographed coastal feature in Pembrokeshire, the Green Bridge of Wales **74** is a textbook example of a natural arch, sweeping across a void and about 80 feet (24 metres) above the level of the sea. There is a good viewing platform near the range boundary fence; from the same point you can see two other arches.

A little way to the east, Elegug Stacks (named after the elegug or guillemot) are also easily viewed from the cliff top. These tall pinnacles of rock, the remnants of past arches, provide safe nesting sites for the largest seabird colonies to be seen anywhere along the Coast Path.

If the 'Range East' section of the national trail is open, you may now continue eastwards on a well-marked path. First you encounter Flimston Castles, basically a peninsula made of near-vertical beds of limestone, but riddled with caves. Across the neck of the peninsula there are two embankments and ditches, indicating that the Iron Age tribe inhabiting this coast enjoyed a room with a view.

The Green Bridge of Wales, a magnificent natural arch on the limestone coast of the Castlemartin peninsula.

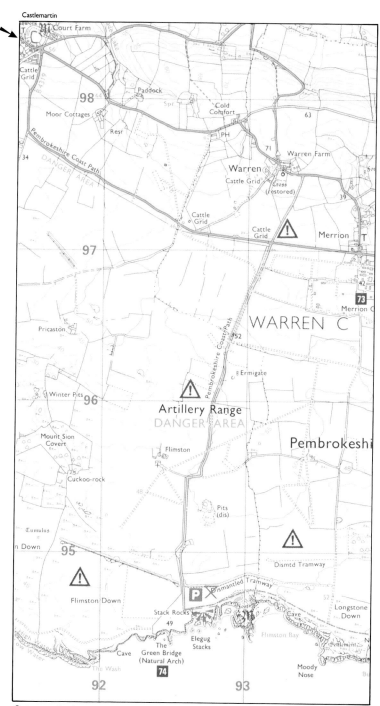

Contours are given in metres
The vertical interval is 5m

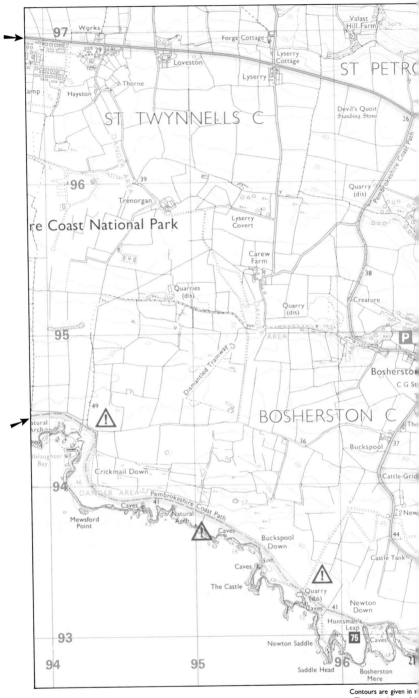

Contours are given in r
The vertical interval i

128

To the east is Bullslaughter Bay; is it named after a laughing bull or a slaughtered bull? There is a guillemot colony in the great gash on the tip of Mewsford Point. From here the official Coast Path runs too far inland to permit good views of the coast, but if you choose to walk along the cliff edge take great care.

As you approach The Castle you may notice a number of caves that are well above the limit of storm waves. Most have now been explored and in one or two there are traces of Stone Age human settlement. Between The Castle and Saddle Head the cliff scenery is superb and includes the feature known as Huntsman's Leap **75**.

Soon you come upon St Govan's Chapel **76**, a diminutive building with an arched stone-vaulted roof, probably built in the 13th century. In recent years it has been carefully restored by the National Park Authority. From the chapel, if you wish to reach Bosherston, follow the road northwards for about $1\frac{1}{4}$ miles (2 km). Bosherston has a few cottages, a pub and a café. The church is a typical Norman structure with a castellated tower, probably dating from the mid-13th century.

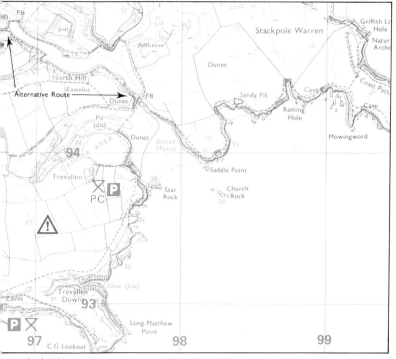

urs are given in metres
vertical interval is 5m

A CIRCULAR WALK TO NORTH HILL, ANGLE

3¾ miles (6.1 km)

Start and finish at West Angle car park or, if you like, Angle village **68**. This is an easy half-day walk, with the possibility of an early retreat from Chapel Bay down to the road. The walk is described anticlockwise. With North Hill on your left, follow the road to and through the village, stopping to take a look at the church, the little fisherman's chapel, and the other ancient buildings. Take the track to the left just after the church, cross the creek and take a look at the fortified tower and the medieval dovecote. Then follow the shore road towards the Old Point House Inn, cross the car park and continue, now on the national trail, to Angle Point and then past the new lifeboat station and along the northern shore of the peninsula. Pass in front of Chapel Bay cottages and behind Chapel Bay Fort. Descend back to the road if you wish; alternatively continue westwards to the cliffs overlooking Thorn Island and swing round into West Angle Bay **69**. Now the path descends gently, passing the old lime kiln en route to the car park, the beach and the café.

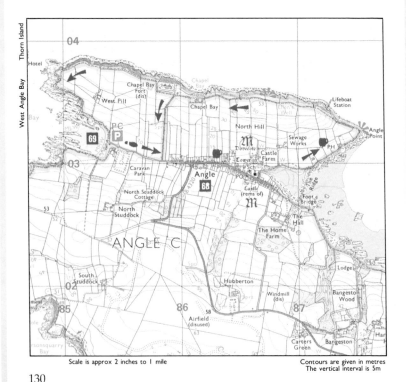

Scale is approx 2 inches to 1 mile

Contours are given in metres
The vertical interval is 5m

Coastal wildlife

The range of habitats along this coast is impressive because of variations in aspect and exposure; cliff profiles, which vary from vertical walls of rock to gently shelving sandy shores; and variations in rock type, which determine soil thickness, acidity and texture. Drainage conditions also vary from place to place; some cliff tops are reached by salt spray while others are not; and the influence of humans and farm animals is locally of great importance. As you walk the national trail, you will encounter vertical cliffs, long cliff slopes masked with broken rock debris, storm-beach ridges, coastal mudflats, sand dune systems, salt marshes, freshwater lagoons, dense deciduous woodlands, as well as close-cropped grasslands and coastal heaths (in spring ablaze with flowers).

There is a succession of habitats in many cliff locations around the coastline. On the cliff faces, exposed to the full force of wind and salt spray, lichens may thrive but other plants seek the protection of gullies and rock crevices. On the cliff top, maritime grassland is at its best in the spring when myriads of hardy flowering plants are in bloom, including spring squill, sea campion, thrift, ox-eye daisy and kidney vetch. Among the earliest of flowering plants are scurvy-grass, violet, celandine, primrose and cowslip. There is always some gorse in bloom, even in the middle of winter. By Whitsun the early spring flowers are joined by bluebell, campion and foxglove, and in May and June you will see spring and summer flowers all in bloom at the same time, with rocky cliff tops transformed into gaudy rock gardens, and areas of grassland supporting brilliant carpets of flowers.

In some clifftop areas there is a variety of coastal heath in which heather, gorse, bracken, blackthorn and bramble figure prominently. As the season progresses, the bluebells are over-whelmed by the vigour of bracken growth. There are scrub bushes and trees (including juniper and oak) in parts of this heathland and on exposed cliff slopes. In a few places sheltered from the westerly winds there are remants of once extensive coastal woodlands, with oak, ash, sycamore, aspen, wild service, beech and many other tree species well represented. The woodlands of Borough Head, Dale and Saundersfoot are typical.

The food resources of the deep clear waters off the Pembrokeshire coast and the abundant safe nesting places on remote cliffs, stacks and offshore islands have encouraged the growth of a large seabird population. On the island of Grassholm there are about 20,000 nesting pairs of gannets, and these majestic birds can often be seen from the trail, fishing close inshore. Puffins and Manx shearwaters nest in vast numbers on Skomer and Skokholm, and there is a sizeable colony of storm petrels on Skokholm. But perhaps the most familiar birds to be seen from the mainland coast are razorbills, guillemots, kittiwakes, fulmars, and various species of gulls. In addition there are colonies and small nesting groups of shags and cormorants, and other nesting species to be seen on the cliffs include choughs, jackdaws, peregrine falcons, buzzards, ravens, feral pigeons, house martins and short-eared owls.

The most important mainland sites for watching cliff-nesting seabirds are the eastern side of Dinas Island (which is of course not an island) around Needle Rock, near the other Needle Rock some $1\frac{1}{4}$ miles (2 km) east of Fishguard, around Stack Rocks and Flimston Castles on the southern limestone coast, and to the west and north of Stackpole Head.

Over the decades there have been a number of changes in seabird distribution around the Pembrokeshire coast, mostly relating to declining numbers as human pressures on the coastline increase. Also, there is the ever-present threat of marine ecological catastrophes, such as that of the *Christos Bitas* wreck, which spilled 2,000 tons of crude oil into Pembrokeshire offshore waters and killed 9,000 seabirds in October 1978. But there are success stories. The size of the gannet colony on Grassholm has steadily increased; the fulmar has spread around the whole of the Pembrokeshire coastline; the local chough population is holding its own; the peregrine falcon population is increasing; and there may also be an increase in the number of nesting sites used by house martins.

We should not forget to mention the other birds that are well adapted to life around the coast. Among the small birds are meadow pipit, rock pipit, skylark, linnet, yellowhammer and stonechat; all are common in open coastal habitats. In the sheltered patches of woodland you will see (and hear) jay, pheasant, wood pigeon, magpie, tawny owl, and even great spotted woodpecker. Yet another group of birds deserves attention, with many waders and ducks using the tidal mud-flats as winter feeding grounds. If you visit the estuaries or the mud-flats of Angle Bay or the Pembroke River you may well see great numbers of shelduck, teal, wigeon, mallard, oystercatcher, curlew, redshank, turnstone, dunlin and lapwing. The mute swan is the largest of the resident birds, but the heron is also very common, and in some winters Brent geese and Canada geese graze the coastal grassland.

Wildlife around the coast is dominated by the birds, but there are plenty of other animals. If you are lucky you may see foxes, and you should look out for badger setts along the whole of the route; otters live close to the footpath in densely wooded valleys, but you are more likely to see rabbits, and hares are becoming more common again after a period of decline. You may see mink, polecat, hedgehog and grey squirrel. Bats are quite common, nesting in many coastal caves and crevices; look out for them at dusk. Adders are also common along the length of the trail, and care is needed if you stray off the footpath and through dry heath vegetation in hot summer weather. Finally, keep an eye open for the less obvious members of the animal kingdom – in particular lizards, newts, frogs, toads, butterflies, moths and dragonflies near at hand, and grey seals, dolphins and porpoises in the sea down below. If you are lucky you may even see a basking shark . . .

Cliff scenery around Linney Head

The clifftop area around Linney Down is made of white reef dolomites, quite different from the bedded grey limestone encountered along the rest of this coast. Once upon a time this was the site of a coral reef or atoll in a tropical sea. Notice the fine blowhole at the end of a deep gash in the cliffs. Linney Head is not as beautiful as it might be, but the view is wonderful and the limestone cliff scenery most impressive.

Pen y holt Bay reveals some spectacular folding structures in the limestones. As you walk across Bulliber Down, Mount Sion Down and Flimston Down, look at the surface of the cliff top. The coastal platform is a classic example of a raised wave-cut platform, in this case 130 to 165 feet (40 to 50 metres) above present sea level. Probably it was formed during a period of relatively stable sea level about 40 million years ago.

11 Bosherston to Tenby

via Freshwater East and Penally
21½ miles (34.4 km)

From Bosherston you have two routes to choose from. It may be possible (firing permitting) to walk south to St Govan's Chapel **76** and continue east along the Coast Path.

If the St Govan's Head section of the national trail is closed by the Army, it is always possible to walk via the car park down to the Lily Ponds and thence via the footpath and footbridges to Broad Haven. The ponds **77** are very beautiful, especially when the water-lilies and early summer flowers are in bloom. Created in the 18th century by the Earl of Cawdor to enhance his Stackpole Estate, the ponds attract innumerable birds. There is a substantial Iron Age fort on the tip of the peninsula between the two western lakes; the site is reminiscent of The Gribin at Solva.

If you are intent upon following the Coast Path, head eastwards from St Govan's Chapel. Soon you come to Trevallen Downs, much disturbed by the Army during the Second World War. If you like, you can take the path cutting off St Govan's Head **A**, but this is not advised – the cliff scenery is too good to miss. The headland itself **78** is riddled with caves, especially on the western flank of the peninsula. The little creek of New Quay is delightful – a deep inlet of crystal-clear water in the mouth of a dry limestone valley with white sand on the sea bed.

As you approach Broad Haven **79**, the Ministry of Defence entrance gate marks the eastern limit of the firing range. If the red flag is flying as you approach from the east, the range is closed and you will have to detour via Bosherston.

Broad Haven **79** is a most attractive beach, with golden sands and a backdrop of sand dunes. At the back of the dune system look out for the bright blue viper's bugloss, the pink and white restharrow (which looks like a sweet pea), and the bushes of sea buckthorn – one of the few plants that local naturalists actually *hate* because it spreads so rapidly and squeezes out other plant species.

The dunes of Stackpole Warren, now well stabilised, are still fed by sand blown up from Broad Haven. This has always been a great area for rabbits, with natural and artificial warrens used by rabbit-catchers until the 1950s. On the coast south of the warren look out for nesting fulmars, razorbills, guillemots and

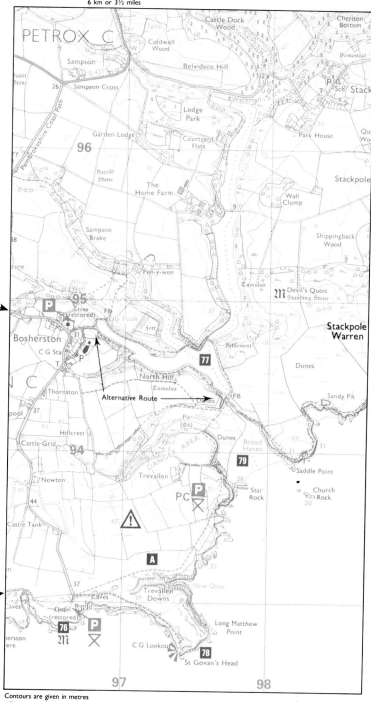

A small lagoon at Broad Haven, near the outlet of the Bosherston Lily Ponds.

choughs. If you wish to take a short route you can cut across the neck of Stackpole Head; however you will miss two huge arches punctured through the headland – the inner one is so high that quite large vessels can pass beneath it. The massive near-horizontal beds of pure limestone provide 'good-quality rock' for climbers, and a wave-cut platform exposed at low-water mark provides access to the base of the cliffs.

Barafundle **80** is totally unspoilt, remote and sheltered from the south-westerlies. The steps and wall on the north side of the bay were built by the Cawdors of Stackpole, and still conjure up images of crinolined ladies flouncing their way down to picnics on the beach. In the area to the south of the valley, excavations by fieldworkers from the Dyfed Archaeological Trust and the University of Wales College of Cardiff have revealed prehistoric field walls, standing stones, Bronze Age settlement sites, barrows and other human burial sites.

Continuing northwards, you soon come to Stackpole Quay **81**, built by Lord Cawdor in the late 1700s inside an old limestone quarry. Limestone was exported by sailing vessels and coal was imported in great quantities for the heating of Stackpole Court, located some way inland above the eastern arm of the Lily Ponds. The National Trust took over 2,000 acres (806 hectares) of the Stackpole Estate in 1976, and careful management is a priority. The Trust has undertaken some interesting and sensitive building conversions near the quay, although the sewage outfall on the beach encourages you to continue quickly along the Coast Path. Soon you come upon a very spectacular contact between the Old Red Sandstone rocks to the north and the Carboniferous Limestone to the south. Note how the cliffs change in colour.

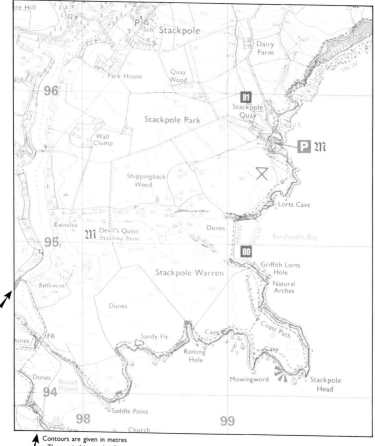

Contours are given in metres
The vertical interval is 5m

Passing Greenala Point you then reach Trewent Point, which affords fine views in all directions. You can either walk across the neck of the peninsula **B** or explore the outer part by a well-worn circular route that is popular with Freshwater East holidaymakers. Do not try to descend the northern slope by any of the smaller paths or you will end in the jungle! Pass Freshwater East **82** by going along the beach or through the dunes to the northern end.

Then you continue eastwards along the cliffs, coming eventually to Swanlake Bay. This is one of the most secluded and least-visited bays in Pembrokeshire, accessible by footpaths via West Moor and East Moor Farms. Like Swanlake, Manorbier Bay has

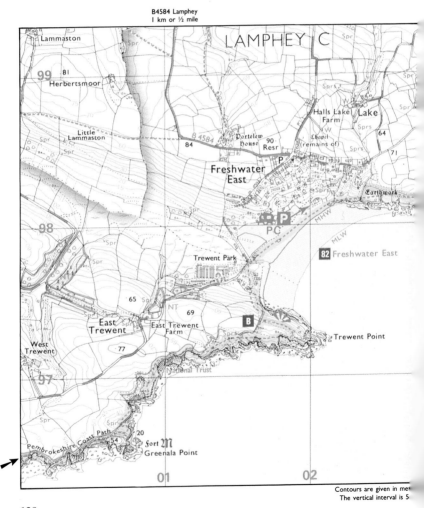

a fine wave-cut platform on its western flank, with a firm, sandy beach near the outlet of the stream. The castle dominates the northern side of the valley and the modern settlement is a little way inland. There is a pretty church with a tall Norman-style tower, and parts of the building are reputedly older than the castle. This was an archetypal Norman manor, complete with priory, dovecote, fishpond, watermill, orchard and deer park. Many traces of this medieval world can still be seen. Gerald of Wales (Giraldus Cambrensis) was born here, probably in 1146, and it is from his writings that we know so much of his home settlement, which he called, naturally enough, 'the pleasantest spot in Wales'.

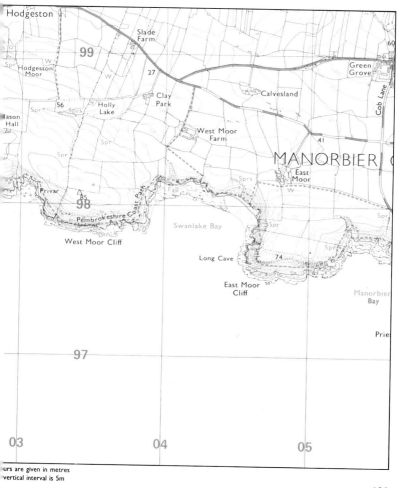

urs are given in metres
vertical interval is 5m

Manorbier Castle, one of the best preserved of the medieval fortresses of Pembrokeshire.

Now you can take one of several paths southwards from the beach **C**, coming soon to the King's Quoit, a Neolithic burial chamber that demonstrates a nice piece of opportunism on the part of its builders. It is adjacent to an outcrop of coarse Old Red Sandstone exposed here in a near-vertical 'wall'. A large slab has fallen from this wall, and has been simply propped up with smaller slabs, providing a convenient burial place. Close to Priest's Nose there are several fearful chasms, up to 70 feet (20 metres) deep, probably caused by the picking out of bands of soft shale between beds of harder sandstone. Be careful when inspecting them. There is an even deeper chasm above the trail; it has sheer sides, and may be 100 feet (30 metres) deep.

Presipe is an attractive bay with clean golden sand, and rocks and stacks projecting through the beach. Access is not too difficult, at either the western or eastern end of the beach.

However, Old Castle Head and its immediate hinterland are occupied by Manorbier Army Camp. The Army has cleared many old buildings, reclaimed some land and released the area between the headland and the housing estate on the main road, permitting a realignment of the Coast Path **D**.

Follow the fingerposts around the fenced perimeter and when you reach the road, turn right and then left at the camp entrance gate. This road will take you to the old army building now converted into a fine modern youth hostel with adjacent camping space. The national trail actually runs a little closer to the coast.

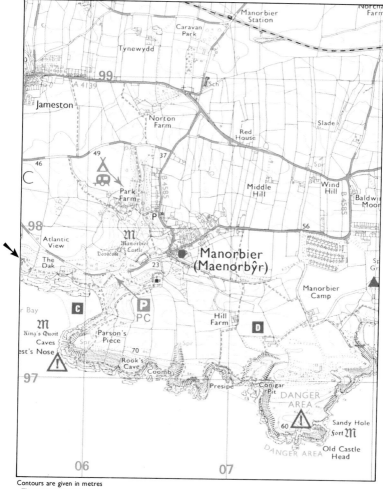

Contours are given in metres
The vertical interval is 5m

Skrinkle Haven **83** is accessible at two points from the Coast Path. There are three beautiful coves here, separated by two large ramparts of limestone that project seawards from the main cliff line. Near the eastern set of steps there is a famous arch in the limestone cliffs called 'Church Doors'. If you descend by the steps remember you have to return, and they are steep! Immediately above, a sizeable area to the east of the youth hostel has been carefully landscaped so that old gun positions have become car parks, viewing points and picnic areas.

At the western end of the Lydstep peninsula, a limestone gorge coincides with a fault in the Carboniferous Limestone. There is a huge blowhole on the eastern flank of the valley, which provides access to the Smugglers Cave. Other caves are accessible at low tide. The National Trust has laid out good, safe paths around the peninsula; follow the long route rather than taking the shortcut.

The limestone coast around Proud Giltar, seen from the beach at the south side of Lydstep Haven.

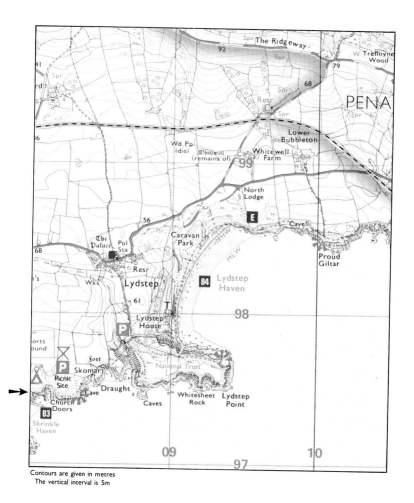

Contours are given in metres
The vertical interval is 5m

Lydstep Haven **84** has formed on the axis of a great east–west syncline or downfold in the Carboniferous Limestone. The beach is a splendid one, and was once incorporated into the elegant Lydstep Estate, with planted woodlands, copses and gardens. Now the place is transformed, with ranks of caravans ranged up the slopes above the beach. Terraces, picnic areas, new roads, shops, car parks and holiday attractions are difficult to landscape, but the holiday company has made worthy efforts and Lydstep Haven could look a great deal worse. You are allowed to pass through on foot. Follow the beach northwards and climb up on to the cliffs at the northern end of the bay **E**.

Continue eastwards via Proud Giltar and Valleyfield Top. Access may be possible on to the small arms firing-range associated with Penally Camp. If so, continue eastwards towards Giltar Point – it is easy walking on springy turf. If the red flag is flying **F**, follow the path towards Penally, passing under the railway and then turning right along the main road. Just past the station there is a right turn **G**. This path leads to South Beach, which you can follow into Tenby. If firing is taking place and this path is closed, continue along the main road then turn right towards the railway line. Walk beside the track until there is a right turn to Bacon's Hole, and from here go on to Tenby.

Penally is a pretty hillside village. The church contains an elaborately carved Celtic cross. Penally Abbey Hotel was once a religious house, and nearby are the ruins of the medieval St Deiniol's Chapel. The village has two village greens, shops, accommodation, pottery workshop and lots of flowers!

Assuming that you can follow the cliff top inside the firing range, continue to Giltar Point. As at Lydstep, limestone blocks

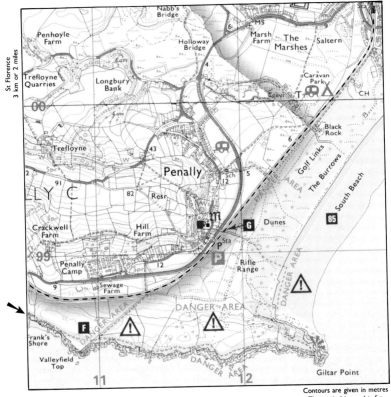

Contours are given in metres
The vertical interval is 5m

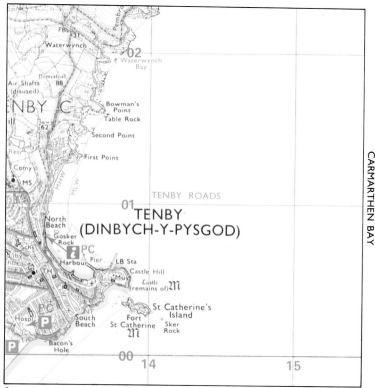

Contours are given in metres
The vertical interval is 5m

could be loaded from the quarry here directly on to sailing vessels or barges that came and went with the tide.

South Beach **85** is a fine expanse of sand, backed by The Burrows. The dunes are oldest in the south and youngest in the north, where they have extended across the mouth of the Ritec Valley since 1811. Sea buckthorn is spreading like a plague over large parts of the northern dune area. The Ritec Valley was once an arm of the sea, providing medieval Tenby with superb natural defences. At that time ships are reputed to have been able to reach St Florence, 3 miles (5 km) inland.

Normally you can walk the length of South Beach on the sand, or along the junction between the beach and the dunes. Then, depending on the tide, you can either climb up the steps into the town, or follow the beach beneath South Cliff towards St Catherine's Island and Castle Hill. There are a number of access points up into the town. South Cliff provides a fine opportunity to examine a long run of limestone cliffs at sea level.

A CIRCULAR WALK TO BOSHERSTON AND St GOVAN'S HEAD

4¼ miles (6.8 km)

Note: access to this walk cannot be guaranteed, since the southern part of it lies within the Castlemartin Range. Check with tourist information centres or with the Range office in case firing is in progress. Assuming that all is well with the world, start and finish at Bosherston, where there is a large car park, or at the Broad Haven clifftop car park. I shall describe the route going anticlockwise from the village. The walk can be completed easily in an afternoon, but you will enjoy it more if you take your time and bring a picnic. Follow the road southwards for about 1¼ miles (2 km) to St Govan's. Take a look at the minuscule chapel **76** and holy well before following the clifftop path eastwards. Examine the superb limestone headland

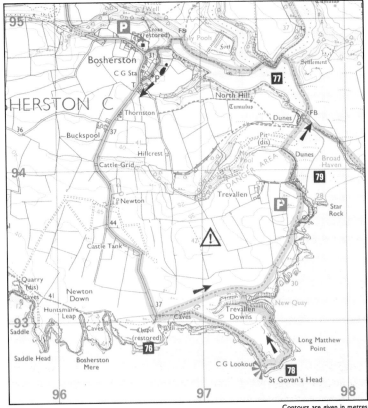

Contours are given in metres
The vertical interval is 5m

Bosherston Lily Ponds, one of Pembrokeshire's favourite beauty spots and also an important wildlife habitat.

scenery **78** if you can; otherwise cut across the peninsula to join the national trail again just to the north of New Quay. Follow the trail to the Broad Haven car park, descend to the beach **79** and swing into the valley towards the outlet of the Lily Ponds **77**. Then you can walk either to the east or west of the outlet; I suggest that you walk along the eastern path, crossing the two footbridges and then walking beneath the fortified promontory towards the car park. Cross the final footbridge and you are soon back at the start.

12 Tenby to Amroth

passing Saundersfoot and Wiseman's Bridge
7¼ miles (11.7 km)

Both Tenby and Saundersfoot are well served by daily bus and rail services. However, if you wish to use Saundersfoot railway station, remember that it is located some way inland of the village and the national trail. Before you leave Tenby, I suggest that you have a look at the town and then resume your long-distance walk by following the good footpaths and roads that trace the cliff line around the built-up area.

The old town of Tenby **86** is tightly constrained within its medieval walls. Parts of the walls are in good repair, although their presence does create traffic problems. The massive South Gate has been knocked about a bit over the years in order to allow traffic to pass through it; the resultant Five Arches form the town's most famous bottleneck. The ruins of the castle can be seen on Castle Hill, which also supports the town's excellent little museum. Other ancient buildings in the town include St Mary's Church, the largest medieval parish church in Wales; the

St Catherine's Fort at Tenby, overlooking part of South Sands.

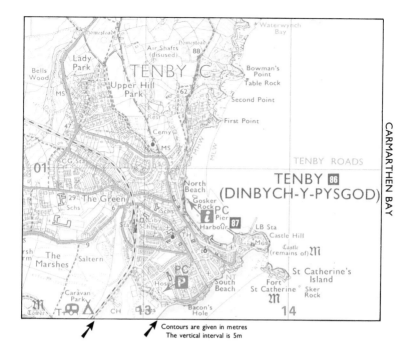

Contours are given in metres
The vertical interval is 5m

Tudor Merchant's House; and the little fisherman's chapel close to the harbour. In Tudor and Stuart times Tenby was an important fishing and trading centre, and there were many powerful merchants in the town. Later the town became a popular health resort.

You can resume your walk on Castle Beach, between St Catherine's Island and the mainland. The island supports a Victorian fort, built in 1868–75 to provide an 'early warning' defence for the Milford Haven waterway. Just above Castle Beach you can see the old lifeboat station, not surprisingly abandoned because of launching difficulties! Follow the foot-path around Castle Hill, making a detour to visit the museum and the castle remains. On the north side of the hill, between the gas lamp standards, are the steps that led to the old Victoria Pier built in 1897. A little further along is the modern lifeboat station.

The harbour **87** is a hive of activity when the tide is in. Follow the Promenade northwards along North Beach, and ascend to the cliff top via one of the flights of steps. Then follow the Croft northwards and continue along the road. The route now takes you some way inland. There are no fingerposts, but head north until you reach the Coast Path proper.

At Waterwynch, a pleasant wooded valley dominated by a view of a large caravan park to the west, turn right if you want to visit the beach. Alternatively, follow the national trail finger-posts through the larch woodland **A**; you will eventually regain contact with the coast. Continue through attractive sheltered clifftop scenery until you reach Lodge Valley, which is thickly wooded with larch and pine. The climb northwards out of the valley is very steep **B**.

At Monkstone Point there are a number of paths to choose from, but views are somewhat restricted by the coniferous woodland. It is possible to descend to the firm sands of Monkstone Beach, but stick to the path and do *not* try to scramble down the unstable slopes **C**. One path leads out on to the headland, and a steep path provides access to the sands near its tip. Once down at beach level, you can scramble across the headland col and (tide permitting) walk on the beach all the way to Saundersfoot. If the tide still permits, you can continue all the way to Amroth (and the end of the national trail) on the sand.

The Coast Path between Monkstone Point and Saundersfoot provides a pleasant walk, mostly through clifftop woodlands. Sometimes it is precariously close to the cliff edge which is hidden by vegetation in places, so be careful. Because the south-westerlies are blowing across land there is no damage to the trees here from salt spray, and these ancient coastal woodlands are the most sheltered to be seen from the trail.

There is access to Saundersfoot beach beside the sewage outfall **D**. If the tide is high, take The Glen road, join the B4316 and follow it through to Saundersfoot. If you descend to the beach, detour a little way to the south to see the famous Lady Cave Anticline (a tight fold in the Coal Measures) before walking north towards the harbour.

Saundersfoot Harbour **88** was built largely for the coal-exporting trade. The village was insignificant until the 1800s, with most of the locally mined coal being exported from the beach. But then the growing demand for Pembrokeshire anthracite led to calls for a proper harbour, and building was commenced in 1829. Many of the local collieries were connected to the harbour by narrow-gauge railway tracks that ran through the village. One of these followed the coast via The Strand and through three railway tunnels en route to Wiseman's Bridge and Stepaside. This is the route followed by the national trail.

The path to the north of Coppet Hall Point continues to follow the route of the old railway track. The cliffs above it are

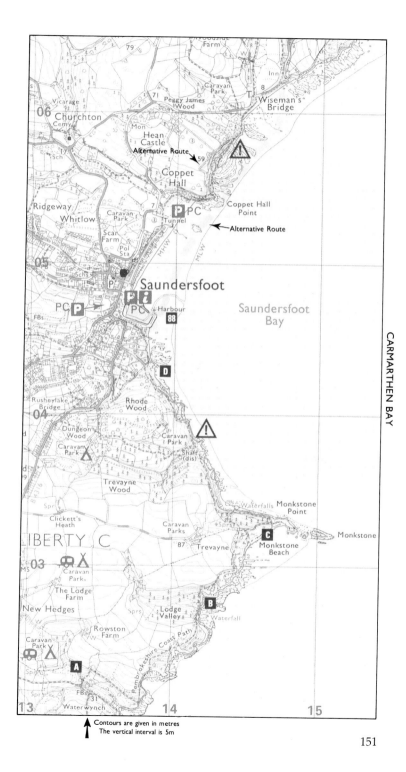

Woodside Farm

79

Inn

8

Caravan Park

T

Wiseman's Bridge

71

Peggy James Wood

06 Churchton

Cemy

Mon

Hean Castle

Alternative Route 59

17

Sch

Coppet Hall

7

Ridgeway

Whitlow

Caravan Park

Scar Farm

Pol Sta

P PC

Tunnel

Coppet Hall Point

← Alternative Route

MHW

MLW

05

Schs

P

Saundersfoot

Saundersfoot Bay

PC P

P i

PC

Harbour

88

FBs

Rusheylake Bridge

04

Dungeon Wood

Rhode Wood

Caravan Park

Caravan Park

Shaft (dis)

D

Spr

Trevayne Wood

Waterfalls Monkstone Point

Clickett's Heath

Caravan Parks

Monkstone

LIBERTY C

87 Trevayne

C

Monkstone Beach

03

MS

Caravan Park

The Lodge Farm

New Hedges

Rowston Farm

Lodge Valley

Waterfall

B

Caravan Park

Spr

A

Spr

FB 31

Waterwynch

13

14

15

Pembrokeshire Coast Path

↑ Contours are given in metres
The vertical interval is 5m

151

notoriously unstable, with ironstones exposed in the Coal Measures. If this route is closed because of rock falls, there is an alternative path along the cliff top **E**, climbing near the hotel at Coppet Hall and descending near Wiseman's Bridge, where there was another coal-exporting beach prior to the construction of Saundersfoot Harbour. Pleasant Valley **89**, which runs inland towards Stepaside, was quite a centre of industry in the last century.

Follow the road past the Wiseman's Bridge Inn, climb the hill and bear right. Eventually the road comes to an end and you are on the footpath again, following an overgrown lane. The path now runs some way inland. As you approach Amroth you must turn right off the track **F** and cross the field, passing into a little patch of woodland, crossing stile 1, and then descending into the village. You have by now successfully negotiated 479 stiles (give or take a few!) since leaving St Dogmaels.

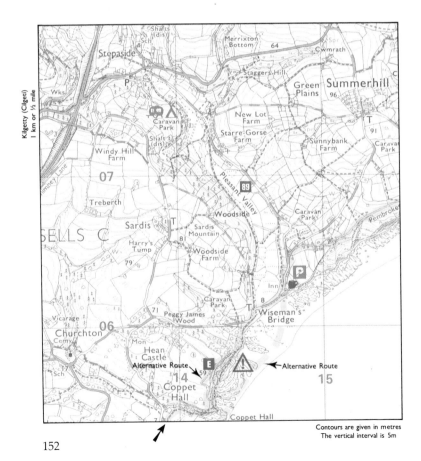

Contours are given in metres
The vertical interval is 5m

The final half-mile or so of your walk is on the road. Amroth **90** is a straggling village, which was originally a small miners' settlement. On the seaward side of the road are the storm-beach and coastal defences; the village wages constant war with the sea, and flooding is a danger when south-easterly gales coincide with high-water spring tides.

Amroth Castle is not a particularly ancient monument. There was a medieval castle here, but it has disappeared without trace; it was replaced by the present building in the 18th century.

The national trail ends at the mouth of the little stream **G** that once marked the boundary between Pembrokeshire and Carmarthenshire. You have now walked, according to the rule-book, 181 miles (292 km). However, if you have followed my advice and explored all the headlands and various diversions along the way, you have walked at least 200 miles (320 km). Now you deserve a rest . . .

Contours are given in metres
The vertical interval is 5m

CARMARTHEN BAY

Storm beach and Coal Measures cliffs at Wiseman's Bridge, near Saundersfoot.

PART THREE

USEFUL
INFORMATION

Transport

Rail
There are good daily rail services between Pembrokeshire and the main South Wales stations, with intercity connections from Swansea and Cardiff to all parts of the UK. The main railway stations are at Haverfordwest, Milford Haven, Fishguard Harbour, Pembroke Dock and Tenby. Other stations are at Pembroke, Narberth, Kilgetty, Saundersfoot, Penally, Manorbier, Lamphey, Clunderwen, Clarbeston Road and Johnston. Stations to Milford Haven have the most frequent services. Stations to Pembroke Dock are served on a branch line via Whitland. Fishguard Harbour trains are timed to coincide with the Fishguard–Rosslare ferry departures and arrivals.

For timetable and other passenger enquiries, telephone British Rail: Fishguard (0348) 782882, Haverfordwest (0437) 764361, Swansea (0792) 467777, or Tenby (0834) 2248. On weekdays enquiries can also be directed to Whitland (0994) 240322. The West Wales timetable leaflet is available from all stations.

Buses
There is a daily express service between Haverfordwest and London, with the express coaches travelling via Milford Haven, Pembroke Dock and Tenby. There are also connecting services to most parts of the country from Swansea and Cardiff. Tickets for all long-distance services should be bought in advance, and bookings can be made through National Express offices or travel agents. For enquiries ring Swansea (0792) 470820.

The main towns are served by good daily bus services, and you are recommended to obtain a copy of the county council's excellent public transport map in order to discover which points on the national trail can be reached by bus. Many parts of the coast can be reached by bus only on certain days of the week, and some cannot be reached at all by public transport. Further information can be obtained from the main bus operators, as follows: Cleddau Bus and Coach Station, tel. Haverfordwest (0437) 763284; Richards Bros, tel. Cardigan (0239) 613756, Newport (0239) 820751; Silcox Motor Coach Company Ltd, tel.

Pembroke (0646) 683143 and Tenby (0834) 2189. Other operators also run services to and within Pembrokeshire, and local time-table information for individual routes can be obtained from the Dyfed County Council Public Transport Information Service on Carmarthen (0267) 233333 ex. 4333, or by post from the Highways and Transportation Dept, Dyfed CC, Llanstephan Road, Carmarthen, SA31 3LZ. The full set of all county bus timetables is available for £1.

Accommodation

Accommodation can be found in all of the main towns and villages on or near the national trail, and in many farmhouses and isolated cottages along the route. Most of the hotel accommodation is to be found in Tenby, Saundersfoot and St David's, but there are many smaller hotels and guest-houses which provide excellent and reasonably priced bed and breakfast facilities for walkers. Remember that you are unlikely to find accommodation if you leave your booking until the last minute and if you want to visit Pembrokeshire at the height of the holiday season; advance booking and planning of your walk are essential. Even simple B & B accommodation in farms and cottages may be difficult to obtain 'on demand'.

The tourist information centres will help you to find accommodation, and all of the Wales Tourist Board centres (Kilgetty, Haverfordwest, Fishguard and Cardigan) operate a bed-booking service. There is also a holiday hotline service for last-minute bookings on Swansea (0792) 645555/645588 (for Wales Tourist Board), on Haverfordwest (0437) 766774 (for Preseli Pembrokeshire District Council) or on Tenby (0834) 2402 (for South Pembrokeshire District Council). For guidance, the coastline north of the Milford Haven waterway falls within PPDC and the coastline south of the Haven falls within SPDC.

The addresses and telephone numbers of the relevant tourist information centres are as follows:

Broad Haven: National Park Information Centre, Car Park, Broad Haven, Pembrokeshire, SA62 3JH. Tel. Broad Haven (0437) 781412.
Cardigan: Tourist Information Centre, Theatr Mwldan, Cardigan, Dyfed. Tel. Cardigan (0239) 613230.
Fishguard: Tourist Information Centre, 4 Hamilton Street, Fishguard, Pembrokeshire, SA65 9HE. Tel. Fishguard (0348) 873484.

The crumbling remnant of Rickets Head on the west-facing coast of St Bride's

...Bay, with St David's peninsula in the background.

Haverfordwest: National Park Information Centre, 40 High Street, Haverfordwest, Pembrokeshire, SA61 2DA. Tel. Haverfordwest (0437) 766141.

Kilgetty: National Park and Tourist Information Centre, Kingsmoor Common, Kilgetty, Pembrokeshire, SA68 0YA. Tel. Saundersfoot (0834) 813672/3 or 812175.

Newport: National Park Information Centre, Long Street, Newport, Pembrokeshire, SA42 0SY. Tel. Newport (0239) 820912.

Pembroke: National Park Information Centre, Drill Hall, Main Street, Pembroke, Pembrokeshire, SA71 4LA. Tel. Pembroke (0646) 682148.

St David's: National Park Information Centre, City Hall, St David's, Pembrokeshire, SA62 6SD. Tel. St David's (0437) 720392.

Saundersfoot: National Park Information Centre, Harbourmaster's Office, The Harbour, Saundersfoot, Pembrokeshire, SA69 9HE. Tel. Saundersfoot (0834) 811411.

Tenby: National Park and Tourist Information Centre, The Croft, Tenby, Pembrokeshire, SA70 8AP. Tel. Tenby (0834) 3510 or 2402.

The main tourism offices are as follows:

Dyfed County Council: County Information Officer, Dyfed CC, County Hall, Carmarthen, Dyfed, SA31 1JP. Tel. Carmarthen (0267) 233333 ex. 4007.

Pembrokeshire Coast National Park Dept: Information Officer, National Park Dept, County Offices, Haverfordwest, Pembrokeshire, SA61 1QZ. Tel. Haverfordwest (0437) 764591 ex. 5135.

Preseli Pembrokeshire District Council: Tourism Officer, Preseli Pembrokeshire DC, Cambria House, Haverfordwest, Pembrokeshire, SA61 1TP. Tel. Haverfordwest (0437) 764551.

South Pembrokeshire District Council: Tourism Officer, South Pembrokeshire DC, Pier House, Pier Road, Pembroke Dock, Pembrokeshire, SA72 6TR. Tel. Pembroke (0646) 684914.

Wales Tourist Board, Pembroke House, Charter Court, Phoenix Way, Enterprise Park, Swansea, W. Glamorgan, SA7 9DB. Tel. Swansea (0792) 781212.

The two district councils publish holiday guides and comprehensive accommodation lists that detail the locations, facilities and prices of all registered accommodation establishments in Pembrokeshire. The Pembrokeshire Coast National Park Authority (address above) also publishes an invaluable *Coast Path*

Accommodation booklet for short-stay visitors; and comprehensive Wales Tourist Board literature on caravan and camping sites, and serviced and unserviced accommodation, is widely available. For a full list of this literature, write to the WTB Swansea office (address above). Pembrokeshire is now well served by regional tourism associations, some of which produce their own accommodation lists. Addresses for the secretaries of these associations can be obtained from the district council offices listed above. Finally, two local guidebooks, *The Pembrokeshire Guide* and *A Visitor's Guide to Pembrokeshire*, contain much information on accommodation. Both are widely available from shops, tourist information centres, guest-houses, cafés and petrol stations.

Camping and touring caravan sites are identified on the Ordnance Survey maps in this book, but such sites come and go, and are carefully controlled by the authorities to ensure that minimum standards are met and to prevent uncontrolled growth in sensitive locations. Inevitably, a number of sites are not shown on the maps, and you are advised to obtain up-to-date lists from the district council or national park offices mentioned above, or from the following organisations:

The Camping and Caravanning Club, 11 Lower Grosvenor Place, London, SW1W 0EY. Tel. London (01) 828 1012.

The Ramblers' Association, 1–5 Wandsworth Road, London, SW8 2XX. Tel. London (01) 582 6878.

Youth hostels

There are eight youth hostels in Pembrokeshire which can be used by members of the Youth Hostels Association. Further information and membership details can be obtained from the YHA, Trevelyan House, 8 St Stephen's Hill, St Albans, Herts, AL1 2DY. Tel. St Albans (0727) 55215. The youth hostels provide cheap and generally comfortable accommodation, but they are irregularly located around the Pembrokeshire coast and not all are on or near the national trail. Also, remember that during the peak holiday period they are very crowded, and advance booking is essential if you are to be sure of a bed space.

The telephone numbers of the Pembrokeshire youth hostels are as follows:

Poppit Sands, St Dogmaels (40 beds): tel. Cardigan (0239) 612936.

Trefin (Trevine) (32 beds): tel. Croesgoch (034 83) 414.

Pwllderi (26 beds): tel. St Nicholas (034 85) 233.

Llaethdy, near Whitesands, St David's (40 beds): tel. St David's (0437) 720345.

Broad Haven (60 beds): tel. Broad Haven (0437) 781688.

Marloes (40 beds): tel. Dale (064 65) 667.

Skrinkle Haven, Manorbier (56 beds): tel. Manorbier (083 482) 31370.

Pentlepoir, near Saundersfoot (26 beds): tel. Saundersfoot (0834) 812333.

Local organisations

In addition to the bodies listed above that deal specifically with tourism matters, there are a number of local organisations which contribute to the protection or management of the Pembrokeshire coast. They all have a role to play, not least in informing and educating the public on matters relating to the coastal environment. They need members and they need financial resources to enable them to act effectively in the protection of vulnerable sites and the encouragement of responsible visitor use.

Council for the Protection of Rural Wales (Pembrokeshire Branch) c/o CPRW, Tŷ Gwyn, 31 High Street, Welshpool, Powys, SY21 7JP. Tel. Welshpool (0938) 2525.

Dyfed Wildlife Trust (DWT), 7 Market Street, Haverfordwest, Pembrokeshire, SA61 1NF. Tel. Haverfordwest (0437) 765462.

Friends of the Pembrokeshire Museums, c/o Curator, Pembrokeshire Museums, Scolton Manor Museum, Nr Spittal, Haverfordwest, Pembrokeshire, SA62 5QL. Tel. Haverfordwest (0437) 82328.

National Trust (Regional Office), The King's Head, Bridge Street, Llandeilo, Dyfed, SA19 6BB. Tel. Llandeilo (0558) 822800.

Other useful addresses

The following organisations are concerned with the protection of the environment or are responsible for the provision of maps and other information.

Conservation Society, c/o RGS, 1 Kensington Gore, London, SW7 2AR. Tel. London (01) 589 5466.

Countryside Commission (Office for Wales), Ladywell House, Newtown, Powys, SY16 1RD. Tel. Newtown (0686) 26799.

Friends of the Earth (Cymru), 3a Lias Road, Porthcawl, Mid Glamorgan, CF36 3AH. Tel. Porthcawl (0656) 715185.

Greenpeace, 30–31 Islington Green, London, N1 8XE. Tel. London (01) 354 5100.

Marine Conservation Society, 9 Gloucester Road, Ross-on-Wye, Herefordshire, HR9 5BU. Tel. Ross-on-Wye (0989) 66017.

Nature Conservancy Council (local office), Sycamore Lodge, Hamilton Street, Fishguard, Pembrokeshire, SA42 0UQ. Tel. Fishguard (0348) 874602.

Ordnance Survey, Romsey Road, Maybush, Southampton, SO9 4DH. Tel. Southampton (0703) 792792.

Royal Society for the Protection of Birds (RSPB), The Lodge, Sandy, Bedfordshire, SG19 2DL. Tel. Sandy (0767) 80551.

Nearby places of interest

This guide has restricted itself to places on or adjacent to the Pembrokeshire Coast Path. However, further inland (and off the coast!) there are scores of sites of natural, cultural or historical interest which are popular with Pembrokeshire holidaymakers. To get a real feel for the character of the area, buy one of the local guide books and obtain a free copy of the National Park's *Coast to Coast* newspaper. Some local guides contain details of inland car tours which take in sites of particular interest. Here is a list of just 20 inland and offshore sites to whet your appetite:

Blackpool Mill An impressive 18th-century cornmill. Machinery still in working order. Now open as a popular tourist centre.

Caldey Island Pembrokeshire's most popular island destination for holidaymakers. Cistercian abbey, ancient buildings, lovely beaches. Regular boat trips from Tenby.

Cardigan Wildlife Park Located not far from Cilgerran, this is an established and popular holiday venue. Many wild animals in large enclosures, nature trail, café and shops.

Carew A lovely, tranquil place, with castle, old tidal mill and Celtic cross in close proximity. Not far away is Carew Cheriton Church, the finest rural parish church in Pembrokeshire.

Cilgwyn Candles Workshop and Mini-Museum This is one of many cottage craft enterprises in Pembrokeshire. Located not far from Newport, the little museum of candle-making history is now a popular holiday destination.

Cwm Gwaun This long and very beautiful valley stretches all the way from Newport to Lower Town, Fishguard. A sub-glacial meltwater channel, it separates the Carn Ingli upland from the main part of the Preseli upland ridge.

Foeldrigarn The finest Iron Age hill fort in Pembrokeshire, located on a summit at the eastern end of the Preseli Hills. Easy access from Croesfihangel, near Crymych.

Haverfordwest The old county town of Haverfordwest, situated right in the centre of Pembrokeshire at the head of navigation of the Western Cleddau River. Castle, ruined priory, old quays and warehouses, fine churches, and Pembrokeshire's best shopping centre.

Lamphey Palace Located not far from Pembroke, this is one of the Bishop's Palaces of Pembrokeshire. Splendid medieval architecture. The buildings are now looked after by CADW, the Welsh equivalent of English Heritage.

Llangloffan Dairy Small-scale traditional farmhouse cheese-making at its best. Visitors can see cheese-making in progress and buy cheeses on the spot.

Llysyfran Reservoir Pembrokeshire's largest water-supply reservoir, built to provide process water for the Milford Haven oil industry. Country park, picnic areas, nature trail, shop/café.

Manor House Wildlife Park One of South Pembrokeshire's most popular attractions, with beautiful wooded grounds, animal and bird enclosures, aquarium, reptile house, etc. Shops, café, picnic areas.

Oakwood Adventure and Leisure Park A very popular family holiday destination, with lots of fun for kids even in bad weather. Various adventure activities, miniature railway, picnic areas, shops, café.

Pembrokeshire Pottery Located at Simpson Cross, this is one of many Pembrokeshire potteries. Visitors can see pots being made. Showrooms, craft shop, and adjacent Motor Museum.

Pentre Ifan Cromlech The most spectacular Neolithic burial chamber in Pembrokeshire, in a lovely setting. The massive capstone (supported by vertical stone pillars) is about 13 feet (4 metres) long.

Rosebush A small settlement with a fascinating history, located on the slopes of the Preseli Hills. Slate quarries and traces of the railway era are prominent, together with relics of abortive Victorian holiday developments.

Scolton Manor Museum An old manor house now transformed into an attractive museum complex. Fine wooded grounds and country park. Frequent events are held in the grounds during the summer.

Skomer Island Skomer is a national nature reserve managed by DWT. The island is magnificent, with spectacular bird life. Visits are most worthwhile during the spring and early summer. Frequent boat trips from Martin's Haven.

Sutherland Gallery, Picton Castle This fine art gallery houses many of the best works of the artist Graham Sutherland. Adjacent craft shop, café and castle grounds open to the public.

Treffgarne Gorge and crags Located in the centre of Pembrokeshire, this is one of the area's favourite beauty spots. River, road and railway squeeze through the narrowest point in the gorge. Up above, on the skyline, are the tors of Lion Rock and Maiden Castle.

Bibliography

The Pembrokeshire coast is well blessed with literature describing it. The list that follows is by no means comprehensive, and new titles appear every year. There are bookshops in all the main towns of Pembrokeshire, and some tourist information centres and other outlets have selections of local books on sale.

Barrett, J., *The Dale Peninsula* (NPA, 1981).

Brinton, P. and Worsley, R., *Open Secrets: Explorations in South Wales* (Gomer, 1987).

Ellis-Gruffydd, I.D., *Rocks and Scenery of the Pembrokeshire Coast National Park* (NPA, 1987).

Evans, R.O. and John, B.S., *The Pembrokeshire Landscape* (Five Arches Press, 1973).

Goddard, T., *Pembrokeshire Shipwrecks* (Hughes, 1983).

Howells, R., *Old Saundersfoot* (Gomer, 1977).

—— *The Sounds Between* (Five Arches Press, 1976).

—— *Total Community* (Five Arches Press, 1975).

Jermy, R.C., *The Railways of Porthgain and Abereiddi* (Oakwood Press, 1986).

John, B.S., *Pembrokeshire* (Greencroft Books, 1984).

—— *The Pembrokeshire Guide* (Greencroft Books, 1990).

—— *Ports and Harbours of Pembrokeshire* (Abercastle Publications, 1974).

—— *Walking in the Presely Hills* (NPA, 1989).

Kinross, J., *Fishguard Fiasco* (Five Arches Press, 1974).

Knights, P., *Birds of the Pembrokeshire Coast* (NPA, 1979).

Kruys, I., *Butterflies of Pembrokeshire* (NPA, 1981).

Miles, D., *Castles of Pembrokeshire* (NPA, 1983).

Amroth Sands, on the north coast of Saundersfoot Bay. This is where the national trail ends.

—— *The Pembrokeshire Coast National Park* (David & Charles, 1987).

Morris, J.P., *The Railways of Pembrokeshire* (Five Arches Press, 1981).

Mortlock, C., *Rock Climbing in Pembrokeshire* (Five Arches Press, 1974).

Pembrokeshire Coast National Park Authority, *Discover the Pembrokeshire Coast* (NPA, 1987).

Price, M.R.C., *Industrial Saundersfoot* (Gomer, 1982).

Roberts, A., *The Best Walks in Pembrokeshire* (Abercastle Publications, 1977).

—— *See the Best of Pembrokeshire* (Abercastle Publications, 1981).

Saunders, D., *A Brief Guide to the Birds of Pembrokeshire* (Five Arches Press, 1975).

Shepherd, A., *A Visitor's Guide to Pembrokeshire* (Guideline, 1989).

Stark, P., *Walking the Pembrokeshire Coast Path* (Five Arches Press, 1973).

Sutcliffe, A., *A Tourist's Guide to the Pembrokeshire Islands* (Anna Sutcliffe, 1989).

Williams, H., *The Pembrokeshire Coast National Park* (Webb & Bower/Michael Joseph, 1987).

Worsley, R., *The Pembrokeshire Explorer* (Coastal Cottages, 1988).

Wright, C.J., *A Guide to the Pembrokeshire Coast Path* (Constable, 1986).

Ordnance Survey Maps covering the Pembrokeshire Coast Path

Landranger Maps (scale: 1:50 000): 145, 157, 158.

Pathfinder Maps (scale: 1:25 000): 1010 (SN04/14)
    1032 (SM83/93), 1033 (SN03/13), 1055 (SM62/72)
    1058 (SM82/92), 1079 (SM81/91), 1102 (SM70)
    1103 (SM80/90), 1104 (SN00/10), 1124 (SR89/99)
    1125 (SS09/19).

Motoring Maps: Reach the Pembrokeshire Coast Path using Routemaster Map 7 (scale 1:250 000), 'Wales and the West Midlands'.

A note to the National Trail Guide user

We hope you like your National Trail Guide.

A great deal of care has been given to accuracy and clarity in compiling these guides but, inevitably, improvements can be made.

To help the publishers in making these books as accurate and useful as possible, your comments and criticisms are welcomed. Please write, giving your own name, address and postcode, and stating which guide(s) you have bought, to the following Freepost address (no stamp required): Countryside Commission, Freepost (GR 1422), Cheltenham, Glos, GL50 3BR.

In return we are offering a new service to you, the user. You will receive a newsletter containing additional information and revisions to help you make the most of the guides and enjoy your walks to the full.